VMware vSphere Troubleshooting

Gain expertise in troubleshooting most common issues in order to implement vSphere environments with ease

Muhammad Zeeshan Munir

[PACKT] enterprise
PUBLISHING   professional expertise distilled

BIRMINGHAM - MUMBAI

VMware vSphere Troubleshooting

First published: October 2015

Production reference: 1261015

Published by Packt Publishing Ltd.
Livery Place
35 Livery Street
Birmingham B3 2PB, UK.

ISBN 978-1-78355-176-7

www.packtpub.com

Credits

Author
Muhammad Zeeshan Munir

Reviewers
Kenneth van Ditmarsch
Péter Károly "Stone" JUHÁSZ

Commissioning Editor
Ashwin Nair

Acquisition Editors
Shaon Basu
Divya Poojari

Content Development Editor
Mamata Walkar

Technical Editor
Mohita Vyas

Copy Editor
Angad Singh

Project Coordinator
Sanjeet Rao

Proofreader
Safis Editng

Indexer
Tejal Soni

Production Coordinator
Melwyn Dsa

Cover Work
Melwyn Dsa

About the Author

Muhammad Zeeshan Munir is a system architect and specializes in the area of data center virtualization and cloud computing. He has been in the IT industry for nearly 11 years after his post graduation in computer science and has been working with Linux, Microsoft, and VMware products. He mainly specializes in designing, integrating, and automating private and public cloud infrastructures for enterprise to start-up companies.

Currently, Zeeshan works at Qatar Computing and Research Institute (Hamad Bin Khalifa University). Zeeshan also provided services as a free lance Assistant Manager ICT Operations to a Milan-based company, Linx ICT Solutions.

About the Reviewers

Kenneth van Ditmarsch is a very experienced freelance virtualization consultant. As one of the few freelance VMware Certified Design eXperts (VCDX), he has clearly added value in virtualization infrastructure projects. He especially gained knowledge and extensive project experience during his last years at VMware and several specialized consulting engagements he worked on.

Kenneth agreed to review this book based on his extensive experience of VMware products. You can check out Kenneth's personal blog around virtualization at `http://virtualkenneth.com/`.

Péter Károly "Stone" JUHÁSZ was born in Hungary in 1980, where he lives with his family and their cat.

He got his MSc degree as a programmer mathematician. At the very beginning of his career, he turned towards operations. Since 2004, he has been working as a general—mainly GNU/Linux—system administrator.

His average working day includes: patching in the server room, installing servers, managing PBX, maintaining VMware vSphere infrastructure and servers at Amazon AWS, managing storage and backups, performing monitoring with Nagios, trying out new technology, and writing scripts to ease everyday work.

His interests in IT are Linux, server administration, virtualization, artificial intelligence, network security, and distributed systems.

www.PacktPub.com

Support files, eBooks, discount offers, and more

For support files and downloads related to your book, please visit www.PacktPub.com.

Did you know that Packt offers eBook versions of every book published, with PDF and ePub files available? You can upgrade to the eBook version at www.PacktPub.com and as a print book customer, you are entitled to a discount on the eBook copy. Get in touch with us at service@packtpub.com for more details.

At www.PacktPub.com, you can also read a collection of free technical articles, sign up for a range of free newsletters and receive exclusive discounts and offers on Packt books and eBooks.

https://www2.packtpub.com/books/subscription/packtlib

Do you need instant solutions to your IT questions? PacktLib is Packt's online digital book library. Here, you can search, access, and read Packt's entire library of books.

Why subscribe?

- Fully searchable across every book published by Packt
- Copy and paste, print, and bookmark content
- On demand and accessible via a web browser

Free access for Packt account holders

If you have an account with Packt at www.PacktPub.com, you can use this to access PacktLib today and view 9 entirely free books. Simply use your login credentials for immediate access.

Instant updates on new Packt books

Get notified! Find out when new books are published by following @PacktEnterprise on Twitter or the *Packt Enterprise* Facebook page.

فَإِنَّ مَعَ الْعُسْرِ يُسْرًا

For indeed, with hardship [will be] ease. [94:5]

This book is dedicated to my parents, who taught me how to write and communicate better!

To my lovely wife. Without her tireless support in different adventures (in UK, Italy, Qatar and Pakistan), I would not have been able to make it!

I would like to thank Dr. Ahmed Elmagarmid (Executive Director of Qatar Computing & Research Institute, Hamad Bin Khalifa University), whose vision inspired me all the way while writing this book.

I would like to extend my special thanks to everyone, including my family (brothers and sister), and friends (Muhammad Imran and Abid) who motivated and helped me achieve this, director, Marco Li Vigni, in Italy whose technical advice and ready support has always been guidance and of greatest value for me.

I would like to thank the reviewers of this book for their feedback and pointing me to the right direction. A special thanks to Mamata Walkar the Content Editor of the book, Divya Poojari, Technical Editor Mohita Vyas, and Shaon Basu for getting this effort completed.

Table of Contents

Preface

VMware has been a famous cloud and virtualization software provider since almost two decades. The VMware virtualization suite vSphere comprises different virtualization producing including bare-metal hypervisors based on vSphere hosts (ESX/ESXi), vCenter Server, vCloud Director, VMware NSX (previously known as vCloud Networking and Security), VMware Horizon Mirage (desktop virtualization), and so on. Virtualization is based on an operating system that can be installed on bare-metal servers and work stations to host other operating systems, for example, Linux, Unix, Windows, and many more. This allows vSphere hosts to share and distribute the available resources (computation, memory, and disk drive) among different hosted virtual machines, and allows them to install different operating systems without exposing the hardware architecture.

Today, many organizations, universities, and research institutes are widely adopting virtualization for day-to-day computing needs using the VMware vSphere hypervisor. Wide growth in vSphere-based infrastructures also requires troubleshooting and resolution of different related issues of the vSphere hypervisor. This is a book that enables system engineers and data center architects to troubleshoot most of the common problems that can be faced in a data center based on the vSphere infrastructure. The book lets you develop a clear and minute troubleshooting approach and lets you adapt to it by practicing it. Real vSphere problems that system engineers may face in the data center are covered by example in this book. In addition to that, vSphere Troubleshooting can be used as a reference and provides a complete overview of the concepts and knowledge necessary for system engineers. You will learn new skills, new tools, and ready-to-use troubleshooting recipes by reading it.

What this book covers

Chapter 1, The Methodology of Problem Solving, covers some of the common troubleshooting skills that can also be applied to troubleshoot vSphere hosts. In this chapter, you learn the installation of VMware Management Assistant (vMA), the first tool to help you get started.

Chapter 2, Monitoring and Troubleshooting Host and VM Performance, teaches you how to use performance-monitoring tools and how these tools can help troubleshoot some very common issues in the vSphere infrastructure. This chapter also covers some of the very important vSphere host metrics and how these metrics can be viewed in performance charts.

Chapter 3, Troubleshooting Clusters, discusses how to get basic information about clusters in order to troubleshoot their common problems. This chapter also covers how this information can be used in advance to prevent any problems from happening. Performance monitoring for clusters is a very important ingredient, and it helps you with your business continuity and managing workloads. The topic on troubleshooting the Heartbeat data store and DRS Storage issues gives a basic insight into some of the very common problems, how to solve them, and some tips for avoiding them from occurring.

Chapter 4, Monitoring and Troubleshooting Networking, covers some of the basic concepts of switching, a deep dive into troubleshooting commands, and some of the tools for monitoring network performance. It also covers how to troubleshoot a single vSphere host using `esxcli` and, for multiple vSphere hosts, how to automate tasks using a scripting language from PowerCLI or a vMA appliance.

Chapter 5, Monitoring and Troubleshooting Storage, covers many different storage troubleshooting techniques, except Fiber SANs. Learning these techniques is a good starting point to manage most storage troubleshooting issues. We also keep focusing on the VMware vMA appliance to deploy our troubleshooting procedures for storage.

Chapter 6, Advanced Troubleshooting of vCenter Server and vSphere Hosts, is where you learn different vCenter Server and vSphere HA agent and state problems. It also covers how to troubleshoot and fix some of the common problems related to vSphere HA. Once you know how to fix some of the common issues, you will get some background of troubleshooting for advanced problems as well.

Appendix A, Learning PowerGUI Basics, shows you how to use the PowerGUI script editor to write your PowerShell scripts. You can use it to manage, not only your vSphere infrastructure, but also your Windows-based environment from a single centralized console.

Appendix B, Installing VMware vRealize Operations Manager, illustrates how VMware vRealize Operations Manager helps you to ensure the availability and management of your infrastructure and applications across Amazon, vSphere, physical hardware, and Hyper-V. You can monitor your applications and optimize performance for your infrastructure.

Appendix C, Power CLI - A Basic Reference, shows you how to download and run the VMware vSphere PowerCLI 6.0 Release 1 or Release 2 in a step-by-step manner.

What you need for this book

This book requires you to have a working setup of the VMware infrastructure, and it should include at least two vSphere hosts in a cluster preferably managed by vCenter Server. VMware Management Assistant (vMA) and vSphere Power CLI are also required to execute different commands and management scripts. Some of the tools can be downloaded from the URLs provided in different chapters.

Who this book is for

The books is intended for mid-level system engineers and system integrators who want to learn the VMware power tools used to troubleshoot and manage the vSphere infrastructure. A good level of knowledge and understanding of virtualization is expected.

Conventions

In this book, you will find a number of text styles that distinguish between different kinds of information. Here are some examples of these styles and an explanation of their meaning.

Code words in text, database table names, folder names, filenames, file extensions, pathnames, dummy URLs, user input, and Twitter handles are shown as follows: "Select the **Deploy from a file or URL** option."

A block of code is set as follows:

```
Writing inode tables: done
  Creating journal (32768 blocks): done
  Writing superblocks and filesystem accounting information: done

  This filesystem will be automatically checked every 28 mounts or
  180 days, whichever comes first.  Use tune2fs -c or -i to override.
```

Any command-line input or output is written as follows:

```
sudo rm /etc/localtime
sudo ln -s /usr/share/zoneinfo/UTC /etc/localtime
```

New terms and **important words** are shown in bold. Words that you see on the screen, for example, in menus or dialog boxes, appear in the text like this: "Select the **Deploy from a file or URL** option."

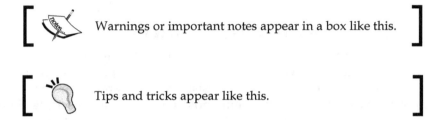

Warnings or important notes appear in a box like this.

Tips and tricks appear like this.

Reader feedback

Feedback from our readers is always welcome. Let us know what you think about this book—what you liked or disliked. Reader feedback is important for us as it helps us develop titles that you will really get the most out of.

To send us general feedback, simply e-mail feedback@packtpub.com, and mention the book's title in the subject of your message.

If there is a topic that you have expertise in and you are interested in either writing or contributing to a book, see our author guide at www.packtpub.com/authors.

Customer support

Now that you are the proud owner of a Packt book, we have a number of things to help you to get the most from your purchase.

Downloading the example code

You can download the example code files from your account at http://www.packtpub.com for all the Packt Publishing books you have purchased. If you purchased this book elsewhere, you can visit http://www.packtpub.com/support and register to have the files e-mailed directly to you.

Downloading the color images of this book

We also provide you with a PDF file that has color images of the screenshots/diagrams used in this book. The color images will help you better understand the changes in the output. You can download this file from: `https://www.packtpub.com/sites/default/files/downloads/1767EN.pdf`.

Errata

Although we have taken every care to ensure the accuracy of our content, mistakes do happen. If you find a mistake in one of our books—maybe a mistake in the text or the code—we would be grateful if you could report this to us. By doing so, you can save other readers from frustration and help us improve subsequent versions of this book. If you find any errata, please report them by visiting `http://www.packtpub.com/submit-errata`, selecting your book, clicking on the **Errata Submission Form** link, and entering the details of your errata. Once your errata are verified, your submission will be accepted and the errata will be uploaded to our website or added to any list of existing errata under the Errata section of that title.

To view the previously submitted errata, go to `https://www.packtpub.com/books/content/support` and enter the name of the book in the search field. The required information will appear under the **Errata** section.

Piracy

Piracy of copyrighted material on the Internet is an ongoing problem across all media. At Packt, we take the protection of our copyright and licenses very seriously. If you come across any illegal copies of our works in any form on the Internet, please provide us with the location address or website name immediately so that we can pursue a remedy.

Please contact us at `copyright@packtpub.com` with a link to the suspected pirated material.

We appreciate your help in protecting our authors and our ability to bring you valuable content.

Questions

If you have a problem with any aspect of this book, you can contact us at `questions@packtpub.com`, and we will do our best to address the problem.

1
The Methodology of Problem Solving

This chapter covers a basic overview of troubleshooting skills, a complete set of troubleshooting tools for vSphere infrastructure, and tips and techniques on how these tools can be used to troubleshoot your vSphere infrastructure.

The topics covered in this chapter are as follows:

- Troubleshooting techniques
- Installing and configuring vMA
- Configuring a centralized syslog server
- Utilizing PowerCLI
- A comprehensive reference of log files
- Collecting logs
- Understanding the health of vSphere hosts

Troubleshooting techniques

We all fix things in our daily lives, and all it takes to fix these things are troubleshooting skills. As with all skills, whether it's playing the piano, fixing a broken car, acting, or writing a computer program, some people are gifted with these skills for troubleshooting by nature. If you have a natural skill, you might assume that everyone else is also gifted. You may have learned how to ride a bike effortlessly, without knowing how much work other people may have had to put into it.

In the same way, some people have a natural talent for troubleshooting and are better at it than others. Such people quickly grasp the necessary steps and easily isolate the problem until they are able to find the root cause. Let's say your motorbike stops working and you take it to a mechanic, telling him the problems and the symptoms of your motorbike. A mechanic who is good at troubleshooting could be able to isolate the problem right away. He could also be able to explain you why your motorbike fails and what is the root cause of the problem. On the contrary, when you take your motorbike to a mechanic who isn't good in troubleshooting, you can expect more time to fix the motorbike and a higher repair bill. You may also need to go every now and then to see the mechanic to get your motorbike fixed at the earliest.

But this does not mean that if you don't have troubleshooting skills, you cannot learn them. Troubleshooting skills can be learned and mastered by anyone. For example, like many other skills, we apply certain techniques in troubleshooting as well — it does not matter whether we are gifted with this skill or not. When we start practicing, it becomes our second nature. We all want to be better troubleshooters, but we also need to be precise and fast. A good system engineer is gifted with troubleshooting skills. When we work in highly available environments where downtime is measured in dollars, we always want to have the right troubleshooting skill set to solve the problem. This requires precision, speed, comprehension, and troubleshooting skills.

Of course, it makes sense that you would prefer to go to the good mechanic who knows what it takes to fix your motorbike efficiently. Applying these scenarios will not only help you to troubleshoot in all aspects of life but also to troubleshoot vSphere in terms of identifying problems and their root causes, and understanding how to fix them.

You should consider a structured approach to troubleshooting rather than doing so without applying any methodology. The following aspects can be helpful and can teach you how to best practice troubleshooting, taking the motorbike to be repaired as an example:

Root Cause of Problem	Troubleshooting Skills Required	In the Engine	Action Needed
Not working at all	Easy	Dead battery	Problem understanding
Malfunctioning	Medium	Dashboard blinking light	Problem understanding + investigation
Malfunctioning, but the symptoms are seen in other components	Hard	Loss of power	Problem understanding + real-time investigation + correlation of events
Not working, but the problem disappeared	Requires on long analysis	Weak battery or some mechanical problems	Problem understanding + historical investigation + correlation of events

Precise communication

You should always establish good communication methods within your work environment. Communicating your problem effectively is one of the key skills required essentially for troubleshooting, especially when you are working in a collaborative environment. Lack of communication can lead to some serious and never-ending problems with increasing down-time. You might be working continuously without realizing that your other team members are working on the same problem as your are. If you've precise communication, you will always avoid the path that your other team members have already discovered.

The following communication methods can be effectively used to communicate within and outside of teams:

- **Direct conversation**: You can communicate the problem directly, in person, with your team members
- **Voice/Video chats**: Voice and video chats are very common now a days and enable a geographically distributed team to conduct regular meetings
- **Web sessions**: Web sessions can be used to access remote systems, conducting presentations and sharing whiteboards
- **Email/Text chat**: Email is the most common tool to used now a days for all kind of office communication

Creating a knowledge base of identified problems and solutions

While working on any system, you will face many common problems again and again. You should always create a knowledge base of these common problems, which includes identifying the problem, its symptoms, and the solution to be applied, along with a **Root Cause Analysis (RCA)** of the problem. Documenting and creating a knowledge repository of these problems and steps taken to troubleshoot them will save you a lot of work in the future. This will also help you to share the knowledge of troubleshooting with all your team members at one place. In addition, it will help you transfer knowledge to your newly hired team members and allow them to use a smarter and more methodological approach towards troubleshooting.

You might be able to fix the issue with no understanding of the root cause, but you cannot completely prevent it. You should always isolate and find the correct root cause in order to avoid problems in the future. If you know the root cause, you can easily assign the problematic issue to the correct team to resolve it accordingly. Sometimes you can come across very complex problems, where you may find the root cause, but sometimes that changes several times in the procedure. Highly available environments also have high stress and require your full concentration, excellent troubleshooting skills, and the correct domain knowledge. This becomes more crucial when it costs your organization money at every single second.

Obtaining the required knowledge of the problem space

For highly available environments, where every second of down time can cost you dollars, you would always have the right people in the right place in order to make sure your investment has been made at the right place. The value you will get by having the right people for the right job would save you not only in terms of **Return on Investment (ROI)** but also in terms of your reputation. If the required knowledge is missing, you should conduct training: first educate yourself and then transfer the knowledge to your team members. A technical team equipped with the knowledge of the problem space is highly desirable at all times.

Isolating the problem space

Whenever you face a critical problem, you should always try to divide the problem into smaller issues and try to divide it among your team members. If your team has only one member, you can still divide the problem into smaller ones. This approach does not only enable you to solve the problem quickly but also engages your team members to concentrate on different areas of the problem. Obviously, you should avoid working on the same problem that your other team members are working on. Thus, you should always make sure you have divided the problem space appropriately.

Documenting and keeping track of changes

You should always encourage your team members to log all their problems, their solutions, and the steps that were taken to reach to the solutions. You could centralize such information using a **Knowledgebase** or a local Wiki within your organization. Once you have your Knowledgebase in place with records of problems and their troubleshooting solutions, you can start testing the solutions. This will assure you that the solutions in your knowledge base are robust and well tested. You can use some kind of document version control so that as the problem evolves, your documentation can keep track of all of these changes.

When you are working in a data center, where you need to work together with other members of a team, this documentation process enables the entire team to solve the problem more easily. If you document the solutions in your organization, you truly enable your junior team members to learn new things and solve problems without involving senior team members.

Troubleshooting with power tools

In VMware vSphere troubleshooting, we will discuss and troubleshoot problems with different vSphere hosts, virtual machines, and vCenter Server. In simple walkthroughs, we will identify the problems and fix those problems by applying our knowledge. You will see how to isolate vSphere-related technical issues and how to apply troubleshooting techniques to those issues. We will discuss different VMware power tools to mange a vSphere infrastructure in centralized way, which includes VMware **vSphere Management Assistant (vMA)**, EXCLI, vSphere PowerCLI, ESXTOP, resxotop, performance monitoring charts, and many other tools. These tools will be introduced step by step in the upcoming chapters.

Configuring the vSphere management agent

VMware vMA is a SUSE Linux-based virtual appliance that is shipped with vSphere SDK for Perl and vSphere command line interface. You can use vMA to manage your entire vSphere infrastructure from a central service console by executing different service scripts, creating and analyzing log bundles, monitoring performance, and much more. You can also use vSphere VMA to act as a centralized log server to receive logs from all of your vSphere hosts. Let's look at the various configuration parameters of our first VMware power tool, vSphere VMA.

Installation

VMware vMA requires a minimum of 3 GB of disk space and 600 MB of RAM. The **Open Virtual Machine Format** (**OVF**) template is based on SUSE Linux 64-bit architecture. vMA supports vSphere 4.0 Update 2 to vSphere 6.0 and vCenter 5.0 and upward. vMA can be used to target vCenter 5.0 or later, ESX/ESXi3.5 Update 5, and vSphere ESXi 4.0 Update 2 or later systems. A single vMA appliance can support a different number of targets, depending on how it is being used at runtime. You will require a user name and password to download the vMA application. It can be downloaded from `https://my.vmware.com/group/vmware/details?productId=3 52&downloadGroup=VMA550`.

We will deploy the new vMA from the vSphere Client tied to a vCenter Server 5.0 or vCenter Server 4.x. It can be deployed on the following vSphere releases:

- vCenter Server 5.0
- vCenter Server 6.0

The virtualized hosts that can be managed from the vMA are:

- ESXi 3.5 Update 5
- ESXi 4.0 Update 2
- vSphere ESXi 4.1 and 4.1 Update 1
- vSphere ESXi 5.0
- vSphere ESXi 6.0

Installation steps

To install VMware vMA, perform the following steps:

1. Once you are done with downloading the appliance, extract the vMA zip file into a directory.

2. Log in to your vCenter or vSphere Client. From your vCenter client, you can select any vSphere host to which you would like to deploy vMA.

3. To start the OVF appliance deployment wizard, choose the option **Deploy OVF Template** from the file menu.

4. Select the **Deploy from a file or URL** option.

5. Then, browse the folder where you have already extracted your vMA appliance. Click on the **vMA OVF** template to select it.

6. Next, accept the vMA license agreement.

7. Give an FQDN to your vMA appliance; I have given mine as `vma.linxsol.com`. The default name is also acceptable.

8. Choose the appropriate folder to store your appliance for inventory.

9. From your vCenter Server, choose the resource pool to allocate resources for the vMA appliance. If you do not select any resource pool, the wizard will place your appliance in the highest level of resource pool, which is selected by default.

10. Choose the storage where you would like to store your vMA appliance; it could be a local data store, iSCSI, FC SAN, or NFS data store.

11. Next, choose **Disk Format** options. I usually choose **Thin**.

12. For the network, you can configure DHCP for your vMA appliance to obtain a dynamic IP address or you can configure the IP address manually. Make sure that your vMA appliance is part of the management subnet in order to access your vSphere hosts and the vCenter Server.

13. By clicking **Next**, you will be asked to review the information. Once you find that the information is correct, you may proceed to click on **Finish**.

14. The wizard will take a while and will then deploy the vMA appliance to one of the vSphere hosts.

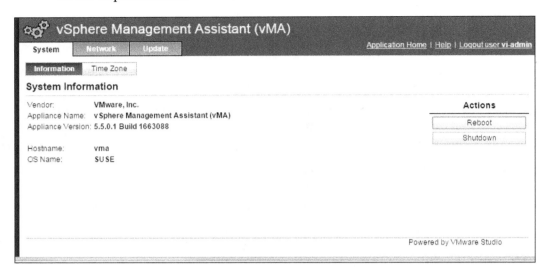

 In case you don't remember the vi-admin password, it is possible to reset it from the GRUB boot loader screen. Choose the very first option **SUSE Linux Enterprise Server 11 SP1 for VMware** and press *e* on your keyboard to edit the line. Move down your cursor to choose the line starting with `"kernel /vmlinuz.."` and press *e* again to edit it. Add `init=/bin/bash` to the end of the line. Then, press *Enter* and press *b* to boot the kernel. The vMA will boot into a bash shell prompt. Next, type the following command to reset the vi-admin password:

`# passwd vi-admin`

VMware vMA features

The vMA is an appliance based on SUSE Linux. It is designed to consolidate vSphere administrative tasks. Here is a brief introduction of vMA features:

- **vSphere SDK and CLI**: You can use CLI to add vCenter Server and vSphere hosts as vMA targets to perform different kinds of operations by running scripts and programs. Adding a target can authenticate you, so you do not require to authenticate against vCenter Server or vSphere hosts when you run an agent or a vSphere CLI command on any of the targets. Do not confuse CLI with PowerCLI, the vSphere PowerShell implementation.

- **Using vSphere SDK API**: You can use the vSphere APIs shipped with vMA to program and to connect to vMA targets programmatically. VMware vMA provides the `VmaTargetLib` library that supports utilization of the API using Perl and Java. You can run agent code using vMA on different software modules and on different hardware supported by VMware ESX. At the time of writing this book, the code can be run only in the CLI of existing vSphere hosts. This agent code can be modified and can be utilized in the vMA appliance by calling the vSphere API.

- **Authentication with vi-admin and vi-user**: The vMA appliance can run agents or scripts that otherwise interact with vCenter and ESX(i) servers without repeated authentication. You can reutilize vMA service console scripts that are presently used for the vSphere host's administration. However, slight changes to the scripts are usually required. vMA comes with two users by default, named `vi-admin` and `vi-user`. To perform all the administrative tasks, for example, addition or removal of hosts, running vSphere CLI commands, agents on the added targets, you will require the user `vi-admin`. To run vSphere CLI commands and agents with read-only privileges on the added targets, you will use `vi-user`.

- **Active directory single-sign-on**: vMA is also capable of joining the MS **Active Directory** (**AD**) domain, and you can use AD user to log in to vMA. This allows you to assign consistent and fine granular privileges to users on the vCenter Server system or the vSphere host, thus enabling users to run the commands accordingly.

- **Vi-logger**: The vMA can collect logs from each of these server types for analysis. This is through a component on the vMA called `vi-logger`.

The vMA consists of the following components:

- **SUSE Linux Enterprise Server 11 SP1 64-bit**: vMA has recently moved to SUSE Linux. Previous versions of vMA were all built on top of Red Hat—either Red Hat Enterprise Linux or CentOS—but with the release of vSphere 5, all virtual appliances have been migrated to SUSE Linux Enterprise Server 11.

- **VMware Tools**

- **vSphere CLI**

- **vSphere SDK for Perl**

- **Java JRE 1.6**

- **vi-fastpass**: This refers to the authentication component of vMA.

Powering-on vMA

You must configure vMA when it boots for the very first time. To do so, power on the virtual appliance. Right-click on the vMA appliance and click on **Open Console**.

You will be presented with a screen prompting for network configuration. To configure network options, you must answer the prompts.

You can also specify the host name for your vMA appliance using one of the prompts. vMA allows you to have 64 alphanumeric characters in the host name.

You must configure a password for `vi-admin`. Answering the password prompt, you must enter your old password first; it will then prompt you to type in a new password. The new password must be able to comply with the vMA password policy, that is, password should be at least eight characters long. It must contain one upper case character, one lower case character, one numeric character, and one symbol.

[The default password of `vi-admin` for VMware vMA is `vmware`.]

AD integration

By default, a vMA appliance comes with PowerBroker Identity Services – Open Edition, formerly known as Likewise Open, to support Active Directory integration. PowerBroker Identity Services uses **Pluggable Authentication Modules (PAM)** and **Name Service Switch (NSS)**. It supports Kerberos, NTLM, and SPNEGO authentication. You can type the following to join your vMA with an AD domain controller:

```
sudo domainjoin-cli join FQDN domain-admin-user
sudo domainjoin-cli join linxsol.com zeeshan
```

The preceding command uses the `Likewise Open`'s `domainjoin-cli` script using the `join` flag, followed by the MS AD controller FQDN and the user name of the user who has administrative rights to join computers to AD. Once you enter this, it will prompt you for a password. Enter the password, and you will see a success message appearing in your console. You can also check the status of your server to see if it has integrated with a domain controller by running the following script:

```
./lw-get-status
```

The script can be found in the `/opt/likewise/bin` directory. You can also check the status of your vMA appliance and AD integration by typing the following command in the console:

```
sudo domainjoin-cli query
```

Either you can append the full path before running the script or you can go to the preceding directory and run the script. The likewise identity service ships up with a lot of different scripts to manage AD integration. You can remove vMA from the domain by running the following command in the console:

```
sudo domainjoin-cli leave
```

The vMA console displays a message stating whether vMA has left the AD domain.

The BeyondTrust website maintains excellent documentation and a community wiki about PowerBroker Identity Services. For more information, please visit `http://www.beyondtrust.com/Resources/OpenSourceDocumentation/`.

 The vMA host name can be changed anytime. Changing the host name is similar changing it in a Linux host: you only need to modify the `/etc/HOSTNAME` and `/etc/hosts` files. You can also change it from the vMA console by typing the command `'sudo hostname new-name'`.

AD unattended access

We will use the ktpass tool to configure the principal name of the vMA appliance for the service in **Active Directory Domain Services (AD DS)**. The process will create a `.keytab` file containing the shared secret key of the service. The `.keytab` file that is generated by the ktpass tool is based on the **Massachusetts Institute of Technology (MIT)** implementation of the Kerberos authentication protocol. The Ktpass command-line tool authorizes Linux- or UNIX-based services that support Kerberos authentication to use the interoperability features provided by the **Kerberos Key Distribution Center (KDC)** service.

In the subsequent example, you will learn to create a Kerberos `.keytab` file called `machine.keytab` in your current working directory for the user `Sample1`. (You will merge this file with the `Krb5.keytab` file on a host computer that is not running the Windows operating system.) The Kerberos `.keytab` file will be created for all supported encryption types for the general principal type.

To generate a `.keytab` file for a vMA appliance, use the following steps to map the principal to the account and set the host principal password:

1. Use the **Active Directory Users and Computers** snap-in to create a user account for a service on a computer that is not running the Windows operating system. For example, create an account with the name `User1`.

2. Use `Ktpass` to set up an identity map for the user account by typing the following in the command prompt:

   ```
   ktpass /princ host/vma.linxsol.com@linxsol.com /mapuser User1 /
   pass MyPas$w0rd /out User1.keytab /crypto all /ptype KRB5_NT_
   PRINCIPAL /mapop set
   ```

   Here, `linxsol.com` is the name of the domain and `User1` is the user who has permissions for the vCenter administration. Now you have a file called `User1.keytab` file. Copy the file to `/home/local/linxsol.com/User1`. You can use WinSCP and log in as user `linxsol.com\User1` to move the file.

3. You can type the following in console to make sure that the user `linxsol.com\User1` on vMA has the ownership of the `User1.keytab` file:

   ```
   ls -l /home/local/linxsol.com/User1/User1.keytab
   ```

   ```
   chown 'linxsol.com\User1' /home/local/linxsol.com/User1/User1.keytab
   ```

   You should mind the quotes around `linxsol.com\User1` so that bash interprets them as a string.

4. Create a cron job for the `.keytab` file so that it can renew the ticket every hour for `User1@linxsol.com`. On vMA, create a script in `/etc/cron.hourly/kticket-renew` with the following contents:

   ```
   #!/bin/sh
   ```

   ```
   su - 'linxsol.com\User1' -c '/usr/bin/kinit -k -t /home/local/
   linxsol.com/User1/User1.keytab User'
   ```

5. You can also add the preceding script to a service in `/etc/init.d` to refresh the tickets when vMA is booted.

vMA web UI

The web UI allows you to manage the vMA appliance. It does not enable you to manage the vCenter and vSphere hosts from the web interface. You can access the web UI by pointing your browser to `https://<vma_address_or_hostname:5480` and logging in as `vi-admin`. The web interface enables you to perform a system reboot or shutdown. You can check the status of the vMA appliance, set its time zone, and update it to the latest version. In previous versions, you were able to use `vma-update`, but now this functionality has been migrated to the web interface. You can also use the web interface to update the network address setting (IP address, HTTP Proxy) of the vMA appliance.

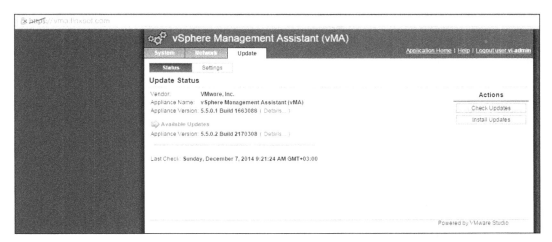

vi-user

The vMA appliance comes with a built-in user called `vi-user`. This user cannot be used until you reset its password. By default, it does not have any password. The `vi-user` user has read-only privileges on the target systems. It also exists on all the target systems by default, regardless of whether you enable it in your vMA appliance or not. You can log in to your vMA appliance by using `vi-user`, but you will only be able to run the commands on target systems that do not need administrative permissions. The `vi-user` user is limited to run commands only against the vSphere hosts that set up with `vi-fastpass` authentication (we will discuss `fpauth` and `adauth` later in the chapter). The `vi-user` user cannot be used to run commands against systems authenticated against AD. It is also unable to run any commands as `sudo`. You can change its password as you change it in Linux normally, by typing the following command in vMA console:

```
sudo passwd vi-user
```

Type the new password for `vi-user` and confirm it once prompted.

Configuring vMA as a syslog server

A centralized syslog server can save you a lot of troubleshooting efforts. For example, if a remote system crashes, you might lose all the important logs within that remote system, which could help you to troubleshoot issues with the remote system. If you log into a centralized logging system, it can provide you with the most recent logs of that remote system before the system crashed.

We will now walk through how to configure the vMA appliance as a syslog server to centralize logging for vSphere hosts. When vMA collects the logs from your vSphere host, sometimes the logs have the vSphere host timestamp, and sometimes they will have the vMA `Localtime timestamp`. `vSphere` host, which uses UTC as its time zone while time stamping the logs. You can avoid the issue of timestamp difference in the logs by changing the local time on the vMA to UTC, with the following command:

```
sudo rm /etc/localtime
sudo ln -s /usr/share/zoneinfo/UTC /etc/localtime
```

You can also set up NTP servers in your vMA appliance to sync your environment's time. To do so, run the following commands in the shell:

```
sudo zypper in ntp yast2-ntp-client  #It will install ntp client
sudo vi /etc/ntp.conf
```

Add in your NTP servers under the heading # Use public servers from the `pool. ntp.org` project. Configure `ntpd` to start on reboot:

```
sudo /sbin/chkconfig ntpd on
```

Now you can start the `ntpd` service:

```
sudo /sbin/service ntpd restart
```

Make sure your NTP servers are reachable:

```
sudo ntpq -p
```

Log files usually grow large in size; you should always consider well your disk space requirements. It is always recommended that you place all of your logs on a separate disk drive.

You should add an additional disk to the vMA appliance where the logs will be stored. If your VMware infrastructure consists of a large number of servers, you should allocate a big enough disk for that.

After hot-adding the disk to the VM, rescan the SCSI bus of the OS in the usual GNU/Linux way to see the disk. You need to become root to perform this action; otherwise you will get **Permission Denied** error:

```
vma:/home/vi-admin # echo "- - -" > /sys/class/scsi_host/host0/scan
vma:/home/vi-admin # fdisk /dev/sdb
Device contains neither a valid DOS partition table, nor Sun, SGI or
OSF disklabel
Building a new DOS disklabel with disk identifier 0x03e0767d.
Changes will remain in memory only, until you decide to write them.
After that, of course, the previous content won't be recoverable.

Warning: invalid flag 0x0000 of partition table 4 will be corrected
by w(rite)

Command (m for help): n
Command action
   e   extended
   p   primary partition (1-4)
p
Partition number (1-4, default 1): 1
First sector (2048-209715199, default 2048):
Using default value 2048
Last sector, +sectors or +size{K,M,G} (2048-209715199, default
209715199):
Using default value 209715199

Command (m for help): p

Disk /dev/sdb: 107.4 GB, 107374182400 bytes
255 heads, 63 sectors/track, 13054 cylinders, total 209715200 sectors
Units = sectors of 1 * 512 = 512 bytes
Sector size (logical/physical): 512 bytes / 512 bytes
I/O size (minimum/optimal): 512 bytes / 512 bytes
Disk identifier: 0x03e0767d

   Device Boot      Start         End      Blocks   Id  System
/dev/sdb1            2048   209715199   104856576   83  Linux

Command (m for help): w
The partition table has been altered!

Calling ioctl() to re-read partition table.
Syncing disks.
vma:/home/vi-admin # mkfs.
```

```
    mkfs.bfs       mkfs.cramfs  mkfs.ext2    mkfs.ext3     mkfs.ext4
mkfs.minix
    vma:/home/vi-admin # mkfs.ext4 /dev/sdb1
    mke2fs 1.41.9 (22-Aug-2009)
    Filesystem label=
    OS type: Linux
    Block size=4096 (log=2)
    Fragment size=4096 (log=2)
    6553600 inodes, 26214144 blocks
    1310707 blocks (5.00%) reserved for the super user
    First data block=0
    Maximum filesystem blocks=4294967296
    800 block groups
    32768 blocks per group, 32768 fragments per group
    8192 inodes per group
    Superblock backups stored on blocks:
            32768, 98304, 163840, 229376, 294912, 819200, 884736,
1605632, 2654208,
            4096000, 7962624, 11239424, 20480000, 23887872

    Writing inode tables: done
    Creating journal (32768 blocks): done
    Writing superblocks and filesystem accounting information: done

    This filesystem will be automatically checked every 28 mounts or
    180 days, whichever comes first.  Use tune2fs -c or -i to override.
```

Create a directory where the logs will be stored. I used /var/log/esxi-syslog/ and mounted the fresh partition to this location: vma:/home/vi-admin # mkdir / var/log/esxi-syslogvma:/home/vi-admin # mount /dev/sdb1 /var/log/ esxi-syslog. To automatically remount the partition at boot time, add the following line to /etc/fstab: vma:/home/vi-admin # echo "/dev/sdb1 /var/log/esxi-syslog ext4 acl,user_xattr,noatime 1 1" >> /etc/fstab.

If you do not configure the preceding line in your fstab file, you will always need to mount your drive manually after rebooting your host.

The vMA syslog configuration file can be found at /etc/syslog-ng/syslog-ng. conf. The default options usually satisfy most of the requirements for logging. The file is self-explanatory, and you can read it to tune your log server configuration.

```
sudo service syslog restart
```

Creating a logrotate file

It is a common practice to rotate logs on Linux systems. You can create a `logrotate` file to compress and rotate the log files. Use vi or a text editor of your choice to create a file in `/etc/logrotate.d` to rotate and compress logs from `/var/log/esxi`.

```
vma:/home/vi-admin# vi /etc/logrotate.d/esxi-log.conf

var/log/esxi/*.log {          weekly          missingok          rotate
6          compress               delaycompress          notifempty
nocreate          sharedscripts          postrotate               /etc/
init.d/syslog reload          endscript }
```

The configuration file is self-explanatory: the first line tells `logrotate` utility to rotate the log weekly. The second line tells it to keep the six log files. The compression will be for all files except the last rotated log.

The vMA authentication mechanism

The policy found in vMA is a credentials caching mechanism that allows us to connect to ESX(i) or vCenter servers. The mechanisms are of the following two types:

- **Fast Pass Authentication (fpauth)**
- **Active Directory Authentication (adauth)**

The `fpauth` essentially allows us to manage a vSphere host or vCenter Server under vMA by using a `vi-admin` and `vi-user` account. The vMA appliance uses a XOR cipher to obfuscate the passwords of both accounts. Once you are authenticated against target vSphere hosts or vCenter, you can start managing targets and execute either vCLI or vSphere SDK for Perl scripts without specifying credentials every time. That is why it becomes much easier to run a single command against a large number of hosts. In previous releases of vMA, `adauth` was used. You can authenticate against vSphere hosts and vCenter using your Windows AD credentials. I have previously described how we can join vMA with an AD attended or unattended. It requires your vSphere target hosts and vCenter to be already members of AD domain.

As we have already configured it, we only need to add target hosts to our vMA appliance to execute vCLI cmdlets or the `perl` scripts provided by vSphere SDK. These credentials remain saved within vMA until you log out or reboot your vMA appliance. Using `adauth` is much more secure than using `fpauth` and I would recommend you to use `adauth` whenever it is possible for you.

We are ready to start adding hosts in our newly installed vMA appliance. I will describe instructions for setting up and verifying both standard `fpauth` and `adauth`.

Accessing systems from vMA

Let's add our first vSphere host to our vMA appliance. We will use `adauth` to add a vCenter Server system as a vMA target.

Log in to vMA as `vi-admin`. Add a server as a vMA target by running the following command:

```
vifp addserver crimv1vcs001.linxsol.com --authpolicy adauth --username
linxsol\\zeeshan
```

The command is self-explanatory here. The `addserver` directive requires the vSphere host or vCenter name to be added, and the `authpolicy` directive requires the authentication mechanism to be used. In this case, I have used AD Authentication. I will show you later how to use `fastpass` to add target servers. If you do not use `authpolicy` directive in the command, vMA appliance uses the `fastpass` authentication by default. The username directive is optional that takes an authorized AD user name to authenticate. If you do not specify it, vMA will prompt you for the AD authorized user name for the vCenter.

We can verify whether the vCenter system has been correctly added to the vMA appliance by running the following command:

```
vifp listservers --long

crimv1vcs001.linxsol.com                    vCenter      adauth
```

Let's add one of the vSphere hosts using `fpauth` to the vMA appliance:

```
vifp addserver crimv3esxi002.linxsol.com --authpolicy fpauth
```

It will prompt you for the root user password of that vSphere host. Let's verify our hosts in the vMA appliance:

```
vifp listservers --long
crimv1vcs001.linxsol.com              vCenter     adauth
crimv1esxi001.linxsol.com             ESXi        adauth
crimv1esx002.linxsol.com              ESXi        fpauth
crimv1esx003.linxsol.com              ESXi        adauth
```

Before we can run the vCLI commands against any of the hosts, we need to set it up as a target. Run the following command to set the target server (`vifptarget --set | -s <server>`):

```
vifptarget --set crimv1esx001.linxsol.com
```

Verify that you can run a vSphere CLI command without authentication by running a command on one of the vSphere hosts. The following command will not ask you for the credentials; instead, it will use the authentication mechanism to verify against the AD Domain:

```
esxcli --server <VC_server> --vihost <esx_host> network nic list
```

You can easily remove the target by using the following command:

```
vifp removeserver crimv1esx001.linxsol.com
```

Now you are ready to use the vMA appliance to manage VMware infrastructure. I will cover more practical examples in the coming chapters.

vMA scripts samples

You can find different scripts written in Perl and Java in your vMA appliance. These scripts are easy-to-use examples that show you how you can modify `VmaTarget.login()` method according to your target host. You can find these scripts in `/opt/vmware/vma/samples`. For code samples in Java, you can browse `/opt/vmware/vma/samples/java`, and for Perl, you can browse `/opt/vmware/vma/samples/perl`. In the `perl` directory, you can find three scripts and a README file: `bulkAddServers.pl`, `listTargets.pl`, and `mcli.pl`. The README file contains all the information you are required to run these scripts. I will walk you through a brief description of what these scripts can do for you. The `bulkAddServers.pl` can add multiple vSphere hosts to your vMA appliance in bulk. The script can read the host names from a text file provided by you or you can pass the vCenter Server host name in the arguments when executing the script. The `listTagets.pl` script can collect different information about your targets, for example, versioning. The last script `mcli.pl` can be used to run a single command on different vMA target hosts. You can provide a text file or pass the host name to the script in an argument.

PowerCLI

VMware vSphere PowerCLI is a powerful CLI that you can use to perform almost all of your daily administration tasks quickly. A basic reference has been provided in the *Appendix C, Power CLI - A Basic Reference*, section of the book to set it up and run the basic command. It can be used to set up a syslog server; it can also be used to download a `vc-support` or `vm-support` log bundle from VMware vSphere vCenter Server and/or ESX/VSphere hosts.

Connecting to vCenter Server or an ESX/vSphere host with PowerCLI

To run specific vSphere PowerCLI cmdlets and perform administration or monitoring tasks, you must connect to vCenter Server or a VSphere host, and then follow these steps:

1. Launch vSphere PowerCLI.

2. In the vSphere PowerCLI console window, establish a connection to a VSphere host or a vCenter Server using the following command:

   ```
   Connect-VIServer -Server crimv1vcs001.linxsol.com
   ```

3. The output appears similar to as follows:

   ```
   Name                        Port    User

   ----                        ----    ----

   crimv1vcs001.linxsol.com            443     linxsol\zeeshan
   ```

 If the certificate is not trusted, a warning display appears. Depending on your security policy, these warnings can be ignored. Once it is done, it will ask you for a user name and password.

Setting up a syslog server using PowerCLI

We will set up a central syslog for our vSphere hosts using the PowerCLI:

```
Set-VMhostSyslogServer -SysLogServer 'vma.linxsol.com:514' -VMHost
crimv3esxi001.linxsol.com
```

You can also remove the `SysLogServer` function by typing the following command:

```
Set-VMhostSyslogServer -SysLogServer $null -VMHost crimv3esxi001.linxsol.
com
```

CMDLETS reference: `https://www.vmware.com/support/developer/PowerCLI/PowerCLI41U1/html/Set-VMHostSysLogServer.html`.

Setting up a sysLog server manually

Let's configure our vSphere host manually to use a syslog server as part of a post-installation script. You can run the following command in the console:

```
vim-cmd hostsvc/advopt/update Syslog.Remote.Hostname string vma.linxsol.com
```

You can also set this in the vSphere Client by clicking on a vSphere host and then navigate to **Configuration | Advanced Settings**. Here, expands syslog in the tree and enter the syslog server details in the **Remote** field.

vSphere host Firewall Exception for Syslog Ports

You may need to manually open the Firewall rule set for syslog when redirecting logs. It seems that for UDP traffic, this firewall rule has no effect in vSphere host5.0 build 456551, and the UDP port 514 traffic flows regardless.

To open outbound traffic via the vSphere host Firewall on UDP port 514, TCP port 514 and 1514, use these commands:

```
esxcli network firewall ruleset set --ruleset-id=syslog --enabled=true

esxcli network firewall refresh
```

A comprehensive reference of log files

You should always configure your log files properly. Log files are the best way to get invaluable information in the detection of a problem and in troubleshooting issues. In the upcoming sections, you will find a comprehensive reference about your VMware vCenter and vSphere host infrastructure components.

vSphere log files – vSphere host 5.1 and later

When you troubleshoot different issues within the virtual environment, vSphere log files become the most important troubleshooting tool one can have. Not only can you use the log files to find and fix the problems, but you can also use them to avoid these problems from occurring in the future.

Logs for vSphere host 5.1 or later are grouped according to the source component (for more detailed information, please visit the VMware Knowledgebase):

vsphere Log files	Description
/var/log/auth.log	vSphere host shell authentication success and failure
/var/log/esxupdate.log	vSphere host patch and update installation logs
/var/log/hostd-probe.log	Host management service responsiveness checker
/var/log/usb.log:	USB device arbitration events, such as discovery and pass-through to virtual machines
/var/log/vmkernel.log	Core VMkernel logs, including device discovery, storage and networking device and driver events, and virtual machine startup
/var/log/lacp.log	Link aggregation control protocol logs
/var/log/hostd.log	Host management service logs, including virtual machine and host task and events, communication with the vSphere Client and vCenter Server vpxa agent, and SDK connections
/var/log/Xorg.log	Video acceleration
/var/log/dhclient.log	DHCP client service, including discovery, address lease requests, and renewals.
/var/log/rhttpproxy.log	HTTP connections proxied on behalf of other VSphere host webservices
/var/log/shell.log	vSphere host shell usage logs, including enable/ disable and every command entered
/var/log/sysboot.log	Early VMkernel startup and module loading
/var/log/boot.gz	A compressed file that contains boot log information and can be read using zcat /var/ log/boot.gz|more
/var/log/syslog.log	Management service initialization, watchdogs, scheduled tasks, and DCUI use
/var/log/vobd.log	VMkernel observation events, similar to vob. component.event
/var/log/vmkwarning.log	A summary of warning and alert log messages excerpted from the VMkernel logs
/var/log/vmksummary.log	A summary of VSphere host startup and shutdown, and an hourly heartbeat with uptime, the number of virtual machines running, and service resource consumption

For information about sending logs to another location (such as a datastore or remote syslog server), see Configuring syslog on ESXi 5.0 (2003322).

Logs from vCenter Server components on vSphere host 5.1, 5.5, and 6.0

When vSphere host 5.1/5.5/6.0 is managed by vCenter Server 5.1, 5.5, and 6.0, two components are installed, each with their own logs, as described in the following table:

vsphere related vcenter Log Files	Description
/var/log/vpxa.log	vCenter Server vpxa agent logs, including communication with vCenter Server and the Host Management hostd agent
/var/log/fdm.log	vSphere host high availability logs, produced by the fdm service

vCenter log files

The vCenter Server logs are placed in a different directory on disk depending on the vCenter Server version and the deployed platform. Sometimes, logs are pointed to store in a drive other than the system drive. As each log grows, it is rotated over a series of numbered component-nnn.log files. On some platforms, the rotated logs are compressed.

vcenter Log Files	Description
%ALLUSERSPROFILE%\Application Data\ VMware\VMware VirtualCenter\Logs\	vCenter Server 5.x and earlier versions on Windows XP, 2000, 2003
C:\ProgramData\VMware\VMware VirtualCenter\Logs\	vCenter Server 5.x and earlier versions on Windows Vista, 7, 2008
/var/log/vmware/vpx/	vCenter Server Appliance 5.x
/var/log/vmware/vami	vCenter Server Appliance 5.x UI
C:\ProgramData\VMware\VMware VirtualCenter\Logs\ vpxd.log	Main vCenter Server logs, consisting of all vSphere Client and WebServices connections, internal tasks and events, and communication with the vCenter Server Agent (vpxa) on managed ESX/VSphere hosts

vcenter Log Files	Description
`C:\ProgramData\VMware\VMware VirtualCenter\Logs\` `vpxd-profiler.log` `C:\ProgramData\VMware\VMware VirtualCenter\Logs\profiler.log` `C:\ProgramData\VMware\VMware VirtualCenter\Logs\scoreboard.log`	Profiled metrics for operations performed in vCenter Server; used by **VPX Operational Dashboard (VOD)** accessible at `https://VCHostnameOrIPAddress/vod/index.html`
`C:\ProgramData\VMware\VMware VirtualCenter\Logs\` `vpxd-alert.log`	Non-fatal information logged about the `vpxd` process
`C:\ProgramData\VMware\VMware VirtualCenter\Logs\cim-diag.log` `C:\ProgramData\VMware\VMware VirtualCenter\Logs\vws.log`	CIM monitoring information, including communication between vCenter Server and managed hosts' CIM interface
`C:\ProgramData\VMware\VMware VirtualCenter\Logs\drmdump\cluster. xxx\proposeAction.dump.gz`	Actions proposed and taken by VMware **Distributed Resource Scheduler (DRS)**, grouped by the DRS-enabled cluster managed by vCenter Server — these logs are compressed and are inside the cluster folder named `proposeAction.dump.gz`
`C:\ProgramData\VMware\VMware VirtualCenter\Logs\ls.log`	Health reports for the Licensing Services extension and connectivity logs to vCenter Server
`C:\ProgramData\VMware\VMware VirtualCenter\Logs\vimtool.log`	Dump of string used during the installation of vCenter Server with hashed information for DNS, username and output for JDBC creation
`C:\ProgramData\VMware\VMware VirtualCenter\Logs\stats.log`	Information about the historical performance data collection from the ESXi/ESX hosts
`C:\ProgramData\VMware\VMware VirtualCenter\Logs\sms.log`	Health reports for the Storage Monitoring Service extension, connectivity logs to vCenter Server, the vCenter Server database, and the xDB for vCenter Inventory Service
`C:\ProgramData\VMware\VMware VirtualCenter\Logs\eam.log`	Health reports for the ESX Agent Monitor extension, connectivity logs to vCenter Server

vcenter Log Files	Description

`C:\ProgramData\VMware\VMware VirtualCenter\Logs\catalina.<date>. log`
 	
`C:\ProgramData\VMware\ VMware VirtualCenter\Logs\ localhost.<date>.log`
	The connectivity information and status of the VMware Web Management Services

`C:\ProgramData\VMware\VMware VirtualCenter\Logs\jointool.log`	The health status of the VMwareVCMSDS service and individual ADAM database objects, internal tasks and events, and replication logs between linked-mode vCenter Servers

`C:\ProgramData\VMware\VMware VirtualCenter\Logs\Additional log files:`
 	
`manager.<date>.log`
 	
`C:\ProgramData\VMware\VMware VirtualCenter\Logs\host- manager.<date>.log`
	Additional log files for the VMware vCenter Server

 If the service is running under a specific user, the logs may be located in the profile directory of that user instead of `%ALLUSERSPROFILE%`.

vCenter inventory service log files

The vCenter inventory service logs are placed in a different directory on a disk depending on the vCenter Server version and the deployed platform. For vCenter Server 5.x and earlier versions on Windows XP, 2000, 2003:

`%ALLUSERSPROFILE%\Application Data\VMware\Infrastructure\Inventory Service\Logs`

The default location for vCenter Server 5.x Linux Virtual Appliance is `/var/log/ vmware/vpx/inventoryservice`.

 If the vCenter Server inventory service is running under a specific user, the logs may be located in the profile directory of that user instead of `%ALLUSERSPROFILE%`.

As each log grows, it is rotated over a series of numbered `component- nnn.log` files. On some platforms, the rotated logs are compressed.

To collect the vSphere 5.1 vCenter Server inventory service logs, navigate to **Start | All Programs | VMware | Generate Inventory Service** log bundle.

Following are the log file locations for vCenter Server 5.x and earlier versions on Windows Vista, 7, 2008:

vcenter Log Files	Description
`C:\ProgramData\VMware\ Infrastructure\Inventory Service\Logs\ds.log`	The main vCenter Inventory Service logs, consisting of all vCenter Server and Single Sign-On connections, internal tasks and events, and information about the xDB
`C:\ProgramData\VMware\ Infrastructure\Inventory Service\Logs\vim-is-install. log`	Information about the installation of Inventory Service including computer name, operating system revision, the date of installation, and the number of revisions that have been installed or upgraded on the system
`C:\ProgramData\VMware\ Infrastructure\Inventory Service\Logs\ wrapper.log`	Information about the status of the Java runtime environment

vSphere Profile-Driven Storage log files

The vSphere Profile-Driven Storage logs are placed in a different directory on disk depending on the vCenter Server version and the deployed platform. vCenter Server 5.x and earlier versions on Windows XP, 2000, 2003:

`%ALLUSERSPROFILE%\Application Data\VMware\Infrastructure\Profile-Driven Storage\Logs`

The default location for vCenter Server 5.x Linux Virtual Appliance is `/var/log/ vmware/vpx/sps`.

If the service is running under a specific user, the logs may be located in the profile directory of that user instead of `%ALLUSERSPROFILE%`.

vSphere Profile-Driven Storage logs are grouped by component and purpose. As each log grows, it is rotated over a series of numbered `component-nnn.log` files. On some platforms, the rotated logs are compressed.

You cannot view vSphere Profile-Driven Storage logs using vSphere Client or vSphere Web Client. To export these logs, see *Collecting Diagnostic Information* in the upcoming part of the chapter.

vCenter Server 5.x and earlier versions on Windows Vista, 7, 2008:

vcenter Log Files	Description
`C:\ProgramData\VMware\Infrastructure\Profile-Driven Storage\Logs\ sps.log`	The main Profile-Driven Storage logs, consisting of all vCenter Server and Management Webservices connections, internal tasks and events, and information about the storage profile integrity
`C:\ProgramData\VMware\Infrastructure\Profile-Driven Storage\Logs\vim-sps-install.log`	Information about the installation of Profile-Driven Storage including computer name, operating system revision, the date of installation, and the number of revisions that have been installed or upgraded on the system
`C:\ProgramData\VMware\Infrastructure\Profile-Driven Storage\Logs\wrapper.log`	Information about the state of the Java runtime environment

Configuring logs and collecting logs

There are different ways to collect logs from vCenter Server and vSphere hosts. You should configure logs using CLI or vMA, or you can use Host Profiles to configure syslog functionality for a cluster or for similar hosts. (We are not covering Setting up Host Profiles to enable logging). You can use the following ways to gather all the diagnostic information from your VMware infrastructure:

- vSphere Client
- vSphere Web Client
- PowerCLI
- vm-support
- vm-support from vMA

Using vSphere Client

vSphere host 5.x diagnostic information can be gathered using the vSphere Client connected to the VSphere host or to vCenter Server. To gather diagnostic data using the VMware vSphere Client, follow these steps:

1. Open the vSphere Client and connect to vCenter Server or directly to an vSphere host 5.x.

2. Log in using an account with administrative privileges or with the `Global.Diagnostics` permission.

3. Select a vSphere host, cluster, or datacenter in the inventory.

4. Navigate to **File | Export | Export System Logs**.

5. If a group of vSphere hosts is available in the selected context, select the host or group of hosts from the source list.

6. Click **Next**.

7. In the **System Logs** pane, select the components for which the diagnostic information must be obtained. To collect diagnostic information for all the components, click **Select All**.

8. If required, select the **Gather performance data** option and specify a duration and interval.

9. Specify the download location in the next screen to download the logs, and then click **Next**, and on the last screen click **Finish** to finish the wizard. On the last screen, you will be presented with a summary of logs you are going to download.

10. Once the wizard completes collecting logs, it will store them in the location you have specified. The log bundle is named with the current date and time, for example, `VMware-vCenter-support-yyyy-mm-dd@HH-MM-SS.zip`.

Using vSphere Web Client

You can gather the diagnostic information of vSphere host 5.0 and higher version by using the vSphere Web Client. The following steps need to be performed to collect diagnostic data:

1. Log in to the vSphere Web Client using your credentials.

2. Click on the **Hosts and Cluster**.

3. Select a vSphere host, cluster, or datacenter you want to collect the diagnostic information.

4. Click on **Actions**.

5. Choose **All vCenter Actions** and then click on the **Export System Logs**.

6. Click **Next**.

7. You can select the different components of diagnostic logs to be exported in the **System Logs** pane. You can choose **Select All** if you want to export all the logs.

8. You can also select the **Gather performance data** option and specify a duration and interval.

9. Then click on **Generate Log Bundle** and then **Download Log Bundle**.

Using the vm-support tool

VMware has provided a useful tool in order to collect diagnostics information and troubleshooting problems. It is a script-based tool that can also collect the state information of the virtual machines. You can run the vm-support in vSphere hosts or from the vMA appliance. Some of the logs that can be collected using vm-support are vmkernel, host, CIM, virtual machines, security, vpxa, cronjobs, dmesg, update logs, configuration information of the NICs, switches, storage adapters, NAS mounts, multi-path setup.

 Follow the link for more information http://www.vmware. com/files/pdf/techpaper/VMware-Customizing-vm- support-vSphere50.pdf.

Running vm-support in a console session on vSphere hosts

Let's use vm-support tool to generate log bundle in VSphere hosts:

1. Log in to the vSphere host using a **Secure Shell Session (SSH)**.

2. Type the following command and hit *Enter*:

   ```
   vm-support
   ```

3. The vm-support command will generate a compressed bundle of logs and will save it in a file with a .tgz extension in one of the following locations:
   - /var/tmp/
   - /var/log/
   - The current working directory

Once this is done, you can download the logs.

 To export the log bundle to a shared vmfs datastore, use this command: vm-support -w /vmfs/volumes/VMFS_DATASTORE_NAME.

Generating logs on stdout

You can also use vm-support to output logs on standard output stream. For example, you can get all the logs over an SSH connection without saving anything locally on the host.

1. From a Linux machine, log in to the vSphere host and type the following command:

    ```
    ssh root@vSphereHostname Or IPAddress vm-support -s > logbundle.
    tgz
    ```

    The `-s` flag tells vm-support utility to stream the logs on STDOUT, following which you can specify the path and the file name you would like to save your logs in. The vm-support utility will generate the logs and store everything into the specified file.

> This requires entry of the password for the root account, and cannot be used with the lockdown mode.

2. Let's do that to generate log bundle and store into a data store:

    ```
    ssh root@vSphereHostnameOrIPAddress 'vm-support -s > /vmfs/
    volumes/datastore001/logbundle.tgz'
    ```

Using vm-support in vMA to collect logs

VMware has provided a nicely written BASH script to collect vSphere host logs from the vMA appliance. You can download the script from the following link: `http://goo.gl/e1R4Zu`.

The script uses `vi-logger` that is now deprecated to collect the logs from vSphere hosts.

Follow these steps to collect the logs from vMA 4.0 or vMA 4.1:

1. Once `1035911_vMA-vilogger-gatherer.txt` is downloaded to your vMA appliance, rename it as `log_collector.sh` by typing the following command:

    ```
    mv 1035911_vMA-vilogger-gatherer.sh log_collector.sh
    ```

2. Give it executable permission:

    ```
    chmod +x log_collector.sh
    ```

3. Run this command to execute the script:

   `/vMA-vilogger-gatherer.sh`

   An archive of log files is created within the current folder.

We can also collect logs from vMA without using the preceding script:

1. Create a directory to store the logs:

   `DIRNAME=log_collector`

2. Now manually copy the log files by running the `cp` command:

   `cp -r /var/log/vmware/* log_collector/`

3. You can compress the log files by running the following command:

   `tar cvzf log_collector_bundle.tgz log_collector`

For the 4.x version, please visit `http://kb.vmware.com/selfservice/microsites/ search.do?language=en_US&cmd=displayKC&externalId=1024122` to configure vMA to collect logs.

Using PowerCLI to collect the log bundle

PowerCLI is a very powerful and easy-to-use command-line tool to manage vSphere infrastructure. It lets you have complete control by automating, monitoring, and managing your vSphere infrastructure.

Collecting log bundles from vCenter Server

We will now use PowerCLI to collect diagnostic log bundles from vCenter Server. It is very simple and a one-line command to execute. Run the following in your PowerCLI shell:

`Get-Log -Bundle -DestinationPath D:\vCenter_logs\logs`

The output appears similar to the following:

`Data`

`----`

`D:\vCenter_logs\logs\vc-support-nnnnnnnn-nnnn-nnnn-nnnn-nnnnnnnnnnnn.tgz`

Collecting log bundles from a vSphere host

Let's download a vm-support diagnostic log bundle from a vSphere host managed by vCenter Server. Enter the following command:

```
Get-VMHost HostNameOrIP | Get-Log -Bundle -DestinationPath D:\vCenter_
logs\logs
```

The output appears similar to the following:

```
Data

----

D:\vCenter_logs\logs\vm-support-nnnnnnnn-nnnn-nnnn-nnnn-nnnnnnnnnnnn.tgz
```

Collecting log bundles from the vSphere log browser

You can access the log browser directly from the VMware vSphere 5.1 web. The client.Log browser is a plugin that works directly with vSphere 5.1. The log browser can be very beneficial and easy-to-use tool when you are troubleshooting problems. Following are some of the benefits of log browser:

- Log comparison
- Searching logs
- Finding and highlighting keywords

The log browser offers a friendly GUI that you can use to take a snapshot of specified host/vCenter logs. Once you retrieve the logs, you can search, compare, highlight, and categorize the logs based on some specific keywords. You can refresh the snapshots of retrieved and stored logs. The search term then can be highlighted for fast navigation. The admin gets a fast UI with the possibility to have the searched word to appear in color. Once you are done, you can export the logs to a file or as a VMware log bundle.

In the troubleshooting lifecycle of VMware infrastructure, log browser is a very handy and useful tool that you can directly access from the vSphere Client. It installs when you install vSphere, and you do not need to look for any other methods to collect the logs. The only problem is that the log browser is only available in vSphere 5.1.

Let's have a quick walkthrough of the log browser:

1. Log in to your vSphere 5.1 web client using administrator credentials.

2. On the left pane, click on the **Log Browser** option and in the **View** pane on your right, click on the **Select Object** option. This will open up a new window from where you can either choose vSphere hosts or any vCenter in your environment.

3. Once the host is selected, you can choose the log file you would like to view from the **Type** dropdown menu.

4. From here, you can browse different log files from different objects.

5. You can also click on **Refresh** for the latest logs.

Exporting logs

You can export log files using the log browser by performing the following steps:

1. Navigate to the log browser and select an object to browse.

2. Select **Action** and then click on **Export**.

3. Select the type of file that you would like to export.

4. Once it is done, click on **Export**. When a new browser window appears, browse a location to save the log bundle.

Understanding the hardware health of vSphere hosts

VMware vSphere hosts use the **Common Information Model** (**CIM**) instead of installing the hardware agents in the vSphere host Service console. CIM provides some management functions for reporting health information or driver updates. For different installed hardware in the server, VMware provides you with the different CIM providers, for example, HBA, Network cards, Raid Controllers and more. The CIM Broker is used to receive monitoring status from the CIM providers. Once the CIM Broker collects all the status information, it becomes ready to publish all the information, which then can be accessed by APIs.

VMware vCenter Server is capable of presenting this information through the **Hardware Status** tab, where it provides all the hardware information:

1. From the vSphere Client, click on **Inventory** and choose **Hosts and Clusters**.

2. Choose a vSphere host you would like to monitor the **Hardware Status** tab and click on it.

3. Browse to the **Hardware Status** tab; it will present you with all the information about memory, CPU, and temperature. You can choose to view **Sensors, Alerts and warnings**, and **System event log** from the dropdown menu.

4. You can export all of this information by clicking on **Export** on the right top corner of the tab.

The host health monitoring tool enables you to monitor the health of many hardware components, including memory, temperature, CPUs, voltage, power, network, battery, software, watchdog, storage, and so on.

Miscellaneous tools

I will cover some of the very important tools for troubleshooting vSphere infrastructure components in the coming chapters, where we will also go through some other general troubleshooting tools, for example, ESXTOP, resxtop, power GUI, memory dump collector, network dump collector, and so on.

Summary

In this chapter, we went through some very basic vSphere troubleshooting techniques that everyone has and how they can keep improving them. We saw some very great tools that let us troubleshoot and solve problems easily. We walked through a step-by-step installation of vMA appliances and how we could utilize it as a syslog server. We also saw how vMA (VMware Management Assistant) could be used to run vSphere API calls and to run `perl` scripts. Then, we used the PowerCLI to collect logs and configure syslog server configuration in the vSphere hosts. The chapter also covered a comprehensive reference of vSphere infrastructure log files and their locations.

In the following chapter, you will learn how to monitor and troubleshoot vSphere hosts and how to fine-tune your virtual machine performance, and you will obtain a basic understanding of key performance metrics of vSphere.

2
Monitoring and Troubleshooting Host and VM Performance

In the previous chapter, you learned some basic troubleshooting skills and performed some vSphere troubleshooting. This chapter extends those skills deeper by using different monitoring tools to observe vSphere performance and identifies any potential problems that can cause bottlenecks in your infrastructure.

The topics covered in this chapter are as follows:

- Tools for performance monitoring
- Analyzing the esxtop results
- Understanding key performance metrics (CPU, memory, network, storage)
- Using vMA and remote esxtop
- Analyzing vCenter performance charts
- Creating charts
- Configuring metrics
- Configuring logging level for performance
- USB attached virtual machines
- Fault-tolerant virtual machines

The previous chapter thoroughly covered how to collect diagnostic information and different logs from vSphere hosts. Sometimes, the diagnostic information you have collected is not enough to identify the root cause of the problems vSphere hosts are having. In order to investigate such problems further, you are required to use different performance monitoring tools. These tools will help you to collect additional data, which could further help you to identify the root cause and would make analyzing the collected data easier.

Tools for performance monitoring

As already mentioned, VMware provides many power tools to monitor the performance of your vSphere infrastructure. These power tools help you to diagnose different problems of your vSphere hosts and vCenter Server in order to resolve them. Let's take a look at some of the tools.

Using esxtop/resxtop

The main tool for performance monitoring is esxtop, which collects data based on different metrics, for example, host memory usage, network usage, disk usage/IOPs and CPU usage.

Esxtop is just like using *top* in Linux. It has the same look and feel and provides the same kind of information provided by top tools in Linux. Esxtop is a famous tool almost every seasoned system administrator knows about. It can be used in real-time performance monitoring of vSphere hosts, and metrics can be monitored for system interruptions, CPU, network, disk device, disk adapter, and memory, each on a dedicated screen. The real-time monitoring can help you to identify different problems, including latency, utilization, and other errors.

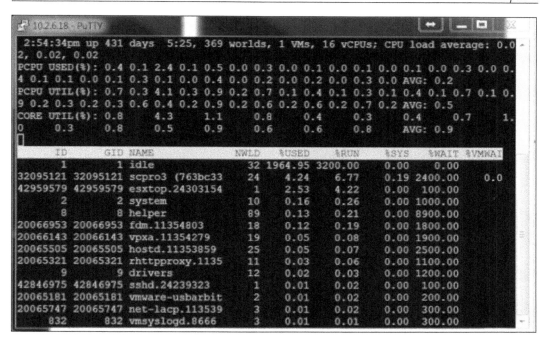

Figure 2.1

There are other tools available from VMware Labs called **Flings**. Though not officially supported by VMware, these tools have been created by VMware engineers to help end users. If you are a fan of GUI, you can use VisualEsxtop, an enhanced version of esxtop/resxtop that can be used in Windows. You can download it from VMware Labs at `https://labs.vmware.com/flings/visualesxtop`.

VisualEsxtop provides you all the statistics that can be collected using esxtop or resxtop. You can use it to connect to a vSphere host or directly to the vCenter Server. The following is a screenshot of VisualTop:

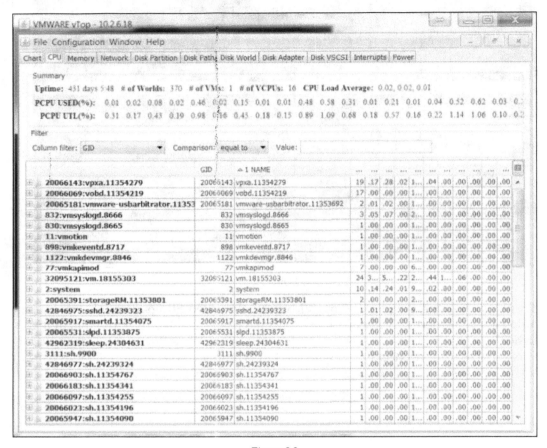

Figure 2.2

Esxtop offers three modes for performance monitoring: interactive, batch, and replay. We will see these modes one by one in detail later in the chapter. For now, all you need to know is that the interactive mode can enable live monitoring of vSphere host performance; the batch mode can be used to export data to other tools for offline viewing; and in replay mode, you can simulate the resources gathered by vm-support.

Live resource monitoring – the interactive mode

As you will notice, esxtop is an extensive but simple tool—it takes some time to get familiar with it. First, I will walk you through this step-by-step, hands-on guide to get familiar with each mode in esxtop, and later I will explain the important metrics used by vSphere host to troubleshoot and tune the hosts' and virtual machines' performance. Let's run esxtop in the interactive mode:

1. Connect to a vSphere host using SSH and log in as root or an administrative user.

2. In the command prompt, type `esxtop` without any flags.

3. It will take you to a statistics console, as displayed in *Figure 2.2*.

4. Let's examine the different screens presented by esxtop. By default, the first screen that appears displays CPU information. You can use the option *c* to see this screen.

5. Press *i* to see the **Interrupts** screen. Press *c* to go back to the CPU information screen.

6. Press *m* to view the **Memory** screen. This screen displays detailed information about memory usage. I will walk you through this in a while in this chapter. Press *c* again to go back to the previous screen.

7. To examine network usage, press *n*. It will show you ports are being used and will present different statistics about network traffic.

8. Press *d* for detailed information about the disk adapter.

9. For disk information, press *u*, and this will take you to the disk information screen. You can find all the information about available storage (local, includes NFS as of 4.0 Update 2, VMFS, iSCSI) to your vSphere host. It will also present the usage, disk read and write, and some other information.

10. Pressing *v* will take you to the disk VM screen, where you can find more information about the virtual machine's disk.

11. Pressing *p* will display the **CPU Power** screen, where CPU power consumption and other power-related statistics can be monitored.

Offline performance monitoring – batch mode

You can also use the batch mode to collect all the metrics and then save it in the `.csv` format. The captured metrics can be examined later for offline analysis using other tools; for example, they can be ported to Microsoft's perfmon or esxplot. The default configuration file of esxtop is named `.esxtop41rc`. You can customize this file according to your preferred list of fields and how they would appear on the screen. The generic esxtop command is written with the following flags:

```
esxtop [-] [h] [v] [b] [s] [a] [c filename] [R directory path]  [d delay]
[n iter]
```

Follow these steps to capture metrics in the batch mode:

1. Connect to a vSphere host using SSH and log in as root or an administrative user.

2. Edit the `/var/spool/cron/crontabs/root` file by typing the following in the console at the end of the current entries:

   ```
   vi /var/spool/cron/crontabs/root
   ```

3. Do not delete the existing entries in the file.

4. In the file, type the following command:

   ```
   30 3 * * * esxtop -b -a -d 2 -n 1000 > data.csv
   ```

5. Save and exit by pressing **wq!** in vi.

6. Once you quit, it will load the new configuration automatically.

7. The preceding command will capture the statistics every day at 3:30 A.M. and write them in a file called `data.csv`. The `-d` flag sets a delay in seconds for sampling, and `-n` sets the number of iterations esxtop should capture. The preceding command collects data after a delay of 2 seconds and collects up to 1,000 iterations. The command will generate data for about 33 minutes for examining.

For vCenter Server 5.5 and later, you can also download ESXtopNGC as a plugin of the vSphere web interface from https://labs.vmware.com/flings/esxtopngc-plugin. This plugin gets integrated with vSphere web interface, and you can directly monitor the performance from the interface without requiring to log in to vSphere hosts. You can find further details on how to install the ESXtopNGC plugin for the vSphere web interface in *Appendix A, Learning PowerGUI Basics* .

Esxplot can be downloaded from https://labs.vmware.com/flings/esxplot.

Replaying performance metrics – replay mode

The last mode of esxtop is its replay mode. We will use the vm-support tool to capture performance data. We have already seen how to use this tool to collect different logs in vSphere. We will use the vm-support tool with –p to collect vSphere performance data. Collecting performance data using this tool is very similar to collecting performance data in the batch mode with esxtop. We need to set up the time interval and length of performance data collection. You can use -d with vm-support command to specify the collection duration and -i switch to define an interval for vm-support to wait between the data collection. To collect performance or diagnostic data using vm-support command use the following syntax:

```
vm-support -s -i 5 -d 10 -w /vmfs/volumes/NFSVol01


/var/log# vm-support -p -d 10 -i 5 -w /vmfs/volumes/NFSVol01


18:37:37: Creating /vmfs/volumes/NFSVol01/esx-crimv3esx002.linxsol.com-
2015-03-26--18.37.tgz


18:41:22: Gathering output from /usr/sbin/localcli vm process list
18:41:55: Done.


Please attach this file when submitting an incident report.
```

```
To file a support incident, go to http://www.vmware.com/support/sr/sr_
login.jsp
```

```
To see the files collected, run: tar -tzf '/vmfs/volumes/NFSVol01/esx-
crimv3esx002.linxsol.com-2015-03-26--18.37.tgz'
```

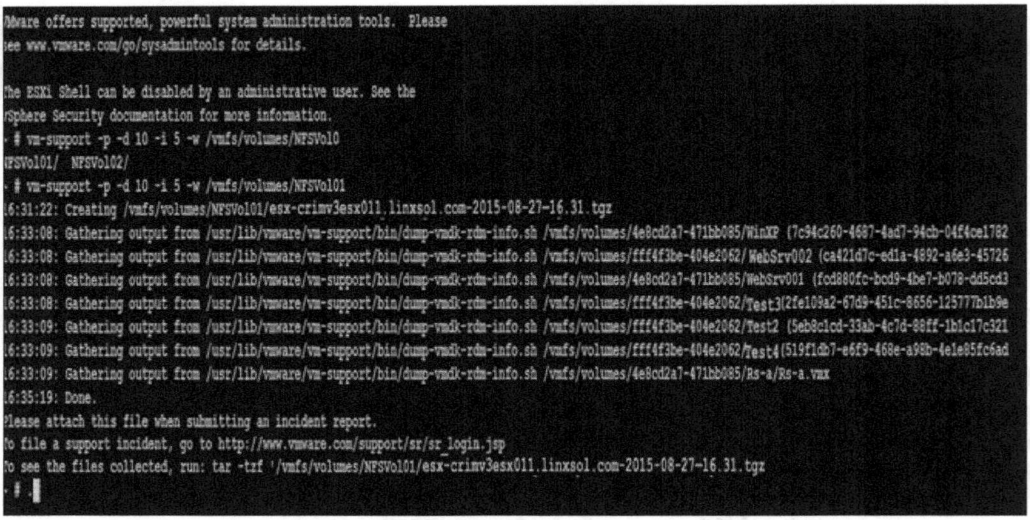

Figure 2.3

The preceding `vm-support` command will gather metrics for five iterations per 10 seconds and a total of 50 seconds. The execution of vm-support will take a few minutes to be completed. Once the execution of vm-support is complete, it will store the file in `/vmfs/volumes/NFSVol01`. The collected metrics are compressed in a `tar` file to save disk space. Use `tar` to extract it so we can use it with esxtop:

```
tar -tzf '/vmfs/volumes/NFSVol01/esx-crimv3esx011.linxsol.com-2015-03—26—
18.37.tgz'
```

Now go into the extracted directory and run the following command:

```
./reconstruct.sh
```

The `reconstruct.sh` command is a script provided by vm-support in the compressed file. This is to avoid the `all vm-support snapshots have been used` error. Now type `esxtop` with the R flag to execute it in replay mode:

```
esxtop -R esx-crimv3esx0011.linxsol.com-2015-03—26—18.37
```

The preceding command will display the metrics from the provided `vm-support` file.

 In VCSA 6.0, VMware has introduced a new tool called vimtop. This is a powerful tool similar to esxtop/resxtop. You can use this tool to monitor and troubleshoot your VMware vCenter Server 6.0 appliance. You can log in to your VCSA 6.0 appliance using SSH. Then type `shell.set -enabled True` followed by `shell` in order to go to the bash shell. Once you are in the bash shell, simply type `vimtop` to get the tool started. If the shell is not the bash shell, you can change it with the `chsh -s "/bin/bash" root` command.

Using Windows Performance Monitor

Now we will use the Windows Performance Monitor tool to examine statistics we have gathered by implementing the preceding hands-on guide:

1. Transfer the `data.csv` file to a Windows computer. You can use WinSCP, a free windows SCP client, to transfer the file.

2. Hold down the Windows key on your keyboard and press *R*.

3. In the **Run** window, type `perfmon` and press **OK** or hit the *Enter* key. It will bring up the **perfmon** tool's window.

4. In the left pane, click on the **Performance Monitor** option. Click on the second icon in the console pane toolbar. It will open the **Source** tab of the **Properties** window for **Performance Monitor**.

5. Click on the log files in the data source and click on the **Add** button.

6. Select our `data.csv` file generated by the esxtop tool in the batch mode and click **Open**. You can also add multiple `.csv` files.

7. You can reduce the range of time you would like to view the data from if you want.

8. Then click on the next tab named **Data**. Click on the **Add** button; you will see the **Add Counters** window. Select **Physical CPU** and **Memory** counters to be displayed, and click on the **Add** button. You can choose other counters if you want.

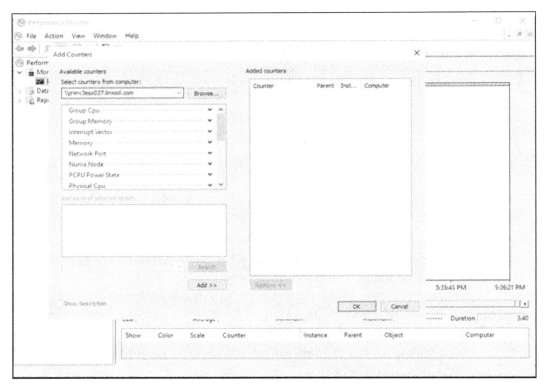

Figure 2.4

9. You can change the graph time by clicking on the third icon in the graph area. You can also generate a report of statistics collected by esxtop.

10. Once you are done with selecting the file or multiple files, click **OK** to close the **Properties** window.

11. Right-click on the **Performance Monitor** display and remove all the counters.

12. Click **Add** and select the desired counters.

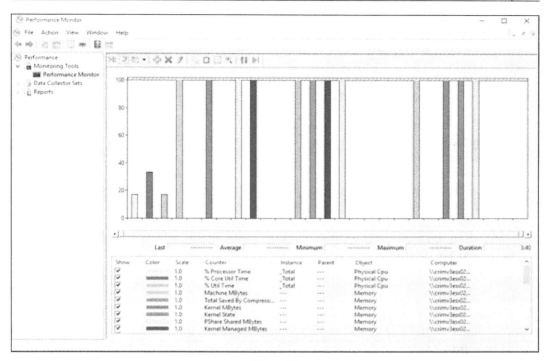

Figure 2.5

Analyzing esxtop results

The data collected by esxtop is processed as rates. When you run the `esxtop`
command without any parameters, it presents the server-wide and individual
statistics of a VM, the resource pool, the CPU utilization, and a world. A world is
a technical term, like a running process in VMware terms, that represents a single
VMkernel schedulable entity or a process or processes running on VMkernel. As we
have a total of 369 worlds (see *Figure 2.1*), it is called **group of worlds**. These worlds
can belong to a group of idle worlds, group of system worlds, group of helper
worlds, or another group of worlds.

Understanding CPU statistics

I will explain the statistics found in *Figure 2.1*. The first line you can find in esxtop or vtop starts with the current system time. The uptime indicates how long the host is up. As you can see in the preceding figures, our host is up since the last 431 days. The next is the number of worlds, which in our case is 369.

The next option indicates the number of virtual machines the host is currently hosting. In the Figure 2.1, it indicates that the host is currently hosting only a single virtual machine. The value 16 vCPUS indicates that the host has 16 virtual CPUs, and the last line indicates the average CPU load. Currently, our load average is 0.02, but if it goes to 1.00 it means that the physical CPUs of our host have been fully consumed. In the same way, if it indicates average CPU load at 0.75, it means 75 percent of the CPU is being utilized by the vSphere host system. If the load average is greater than the CPU cores you have, it indicates that the CPU resources of your vSphere host are overloaded and requires the CPUs to be doubled up.

The PCPU section indicates the percentage of individual physical CPUs. You can see the usage of 16 physical CPUs in *Figure 2.1*. The value of Avg. 05 PCPU shows the total average percentage in all of the 16 CPUs. The ideal usage of CPUs should be up to 80 percent. CPUs are considered overloaded if the average percentage of PCPU reaches 90 percent, but not for all organizations. However, usage of 90 percent and above is clearly a warning that CPU resources are going to be overloaded. If a vSphere host is installed on a machine enabled with hyper-threading, the PCPU field also displays information about the logical CPU (LCPU) usage. If a vSphere host in a cluster fails, vSphere HA will try to start the virtual machines for the other available vSphere hosts, but if the CPU resources on the vSphere hosts are already exhausted, your virtual machines will not be powered on.

The rest of the metrics are presented in the table in the next section, and most of them are self-explanatory. The CPU panel can be customized using single-key commands as you do in the top tool in Linux or Windows.

Enabling more esxtop fields

You can perform the following steps in order to choose more fields for the CPU screen:

1. Press *f* to enter another screen called the **Current Field Order** screen.

2. You can toggle any of the fields you would like to display. The field order starts from A to J.

3. For this exercise, press *I* to choose **CPU Summary Statistics**.

4. Press *Esc* to get back to the CPU statistics screen. You will see that the number of columns has increased.

The same procedure can be adopted for other statistics screens, for example memory, network, or disk screens. You can also use *e* for extended statistics about a group. Press *e* while esxtop is running in the interactive mode. Enter the **Group ID (GID)** for which you would like to see the extended statistics, and esxtop will display the extended information about that resource group.

Pressing *U* will sort all the resources by utilization; pressing *R* will sort all the resources by %RDY (see *Table – 2.1 CPU Metrics*) state. Pressing *V* will display resources relevant to virtual machines, and *N* will sort them by the GID column.

Hit *h* anytime in esxtop interactive mode for the help menu. Use `extop -l` to lock particular resources and it will bind esxtop to utilize the needed amount of CPU power.

Table – 2.1 CPU Metrics

CPU Metrics	Description
PCPU USED	The PCPU USED field shows the percentage of execution of a resource by a physical CPU. You can monitor the percentage of all physical CPUs separately. It will start from CPU0, CPU1, and so on, up to CPUn. You can also monitor the average percentage at the end of the line. According to advice from VMWare, the average load percentage of 80.00 is an ideal usage percentage. The CPUs will be considered overloaded if that percentage starts reaching 90 percent or goes above.
PCPU UTIL	PCPU UTIL presents the percentage of time when the PCPU is actually being utilized or is in the busy state.
CORE UTIL	The CORE UTIL field is not available if your system doesn't support hyper-threading. The CORE UTIL field represents the percentage of time a CPU core is being utilized.
ID	ID represents a resource ID running in the vSphere host system. That resource could be a world, a virtual machine, or a resource pool.
GID Name	The GID Name could be a Virtual Machine ID of a world or resource pool, a group ID, or a resource pool ID.
NWLD	Num Members of a resource pool or a vm.
%USED	This defines how many CPU core cycles are being utilized by different resources.

CPU Metrics	Description
%RUN	This shows the percentage of the entire duration which is scheduled.
%SYS	The percentage of Sys time is used to compute %USED. The percentage of Sys shows how much time has been spent in VMkernel for VMs or resource pools to respond to interrupts and to process other system activities. The high values in this field mean high I/O requests. You would not like to see this value higher than 20.
%WAIT	WAIT percentage time explains how much time a process has spent in the state of waiting. The process could be a VM, a resource pool, or a world. The WAIT percentage also sums up the percentage of a process' idle state.
%VMWAIT	VMWAIT is only applicable to the vCPU worlds of a virtual machine. VMWAIT doesn't sum up the idle time. It only explains how much a virtual machine is in the blocked state.
%RDY	The resources (VMs, world, resource pools) are put in the RDY state for running but waiting to execute for CPU resources to be provided. You can monitor it to identify vCPU overuse. The threshold for %RDY is 10.
%IDLE	IDLE indicates the percentage of time a resource is in the idle state.
%OVRLP	This is the percentage of duration that a system takes to schedule a resource (VMs, world, resource pools) in place of another resource (for example, another VM or resource pool).
%CSTP	This is for internal use of VMware. You can use it to identify the excessive use of vSMP. Reducing the number of vCPUs can avoid this problem. The threshold value for %CSTP is 3.
%MLMTD	This is the percentage of time a resource is ready to run, but it may violate the CPU limit set and is not being scheduled. The threshold value for %MLMTD is 0. Values larger than the threshold values mean a limit has been set.
%SWPWT	%SWPWT indicates the percentage of duration a world waits for the VMkernel swapping memory.

Memory statistics

VMware vSphere hosts are designed to utilize memory efficiently like other resources. The resource management policies are implemented in the vSphere host to allocate memory to the virtual machines it is hosting. This allocation is based on the allocated memory setting of a virtual machine and the current system load. The vSphere host reveals different memory statistics that can be viewed using esxtop. Before we start looking into memory statistics, let's look at a brief introduction of how a vSphere host manages its memory.

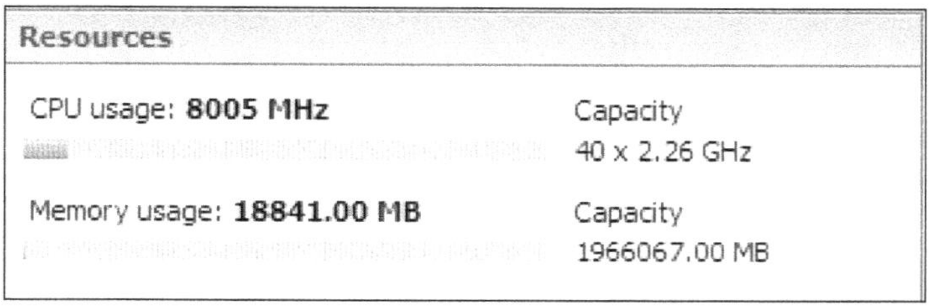

Figure 2.6

Memory management in a vSphere host

Before we take a look at vSphere host memory metrics, I will walk you through memory management in a vSphere host system briefly. The memory management concept in a vSphere host will help you to understand the metrics displayed by esxtop. A vSphere host reclaims memory to provision memory overcommitment.

Memory overcommitment

The vSphere host system reserves physical memory for guaranteed delivery of memory to all the running virtual machines. The system uses the technique of overcommitting in order to ensure that it can allocate more memory than its capacity. The memory of a vSphere host is considered to be overcommitted when the total amount of virtual machine physical memory increases the total amount of the vSphere host. You can understand memory overcommitting through this example: let's say you have a host with 8 GB of physical memory and you are running five virtual machines with 2 GB each. The overcommitment of memory allows the vSphere host system to improve and balance the memory usage of physical memory. I will not discuss this in further detail as this is out of the scope of this book.

Memory overhead

Virtual machines have two types of memory overhead: the extra time (time overhead) to access a virtual machine's memory and a specific amount of overhead memory that is required to power on virtual machines. The total amount of memory for a virtual machine depends on the number of vCPUs, allocated memory, and the overhead memory for that virtual machine. Once the virtual machine starts running, the overhead memory varies than shown in *Table – 2.1*.

Total memory for 1 vCPU VM = allocated memory + overhead memory

You should have knowledge of this overhead to troubleshoot memory overhead problems. The following table has been taken from the VMware vSphere 5.1 documentation, and the sample values in the table have been collected with MMU enabled for virtual machines. These overhead values can be slightly different than those listed in the table.

Table - 2.2 Memory Overhead for each VCPU

Memory (MB)	1 VCPU	2 VCPUs	4 VCPUs	8 VCPUs
256	20.29	24.28	32.23	48.16
1024	25.90	29.91	37.86	53.82
4096	48.64	52.72	60.67	76.78
16384	139.62	143.98	151.93	168.60

Transparent page sharing

I will briefly describe **transparent page sharing** (TPS). VMware ESXi systems can efficiently use physical memory using TPS. Let's say you have some of your virtual machines running a common OS; some of these can have the same blocks of memory. The ESXi host can use the TPS to reclaim the identical pages of memory and keep a single memory page to share among all the virtual machines. This results in better host memory consumption and the host attains better memory overcommitment.

> TPS is enabled by default in all vSphere versions, except in the 5.0, 5.1, 5.5 updates. In the future releases of vSphere (version 6.0 and above), TPS will be disabled by default. The TPS setting can be enabled from vSphere Advanced Settings.

Ballooning

Ballooning is a memory reclamation technique that dispatches a message to running virtual machines stating that the hypervisor is low on memory. A vSphere host uses a memory balloon driver called `vmmemctl` installed with VMware tools in the guest virtual machines to reclaim the free memory. When a vSphere host needs to reclaim the virtual machine memory, it uses the memory balloon driver `vmmemctl` to do it. The memory balloon driver `vmmemctl` creates a balloon size for the driver by expanding the balloon and allocating guest physical pages in the guest virtual machines to reclaim the memory. The driver tries to reclaim memory pages that it believes are less valuable for the guest operating system using appropriate ballooning techniques.

Memory compression

VMware vSphere hosts use a compression cache within physical memory to save pages instead of swapping these pages out to the disk. Memory compression provides a better method of page swapping because the host only needs to decompress a page directly from memory instead of accessing a disk, which is slower.

Reference: `http://www.vmware.com/files/pdf/mem_mgmt_perf_vsphere5.pdf`

Esxtop for memory statistics

Let's use esxtop to view memory metrics:

1. Connect to a vSphere host using SSH and log in as root or an administrative user.

2. In the command prompt, type `esxtop` without any flags.

3. Press *m* to go to the memory screen. This screen displays detailed information about memory usage.

4. Enable some additional memory statistics fields in esxtop for the following field: `MCTL`.

5. Press *f* to go to the **Current Field Order** screen.

6. Press *j* to enable MCTL memory statistics, and press it again to remove this field.

7. Press the *Esc* key to return to the esxtop memory statistics screen.

```
10:56:12am up 438 days 1:26, 370 worlds, 1 VMs, 16 vCPUs; MEM overcommit avg: 0.00, 0.00, 0.00
PMEM  /MB: 262098    total:  2677    vmk,131862 other, 127558 free
VMKMEM/MB: 261714 managed:  3231 minfree, 139761 rsvd, 121952 ursvd,  high state
NUMA  /MB: 131026 (60381), 131072 (66792)
PSHARE/MB:    20 shared,    20 common:     0 saving
SWAP  /MB:     0   curr,     0 rclmtgt:            0.00 r/s,   0.00 w/s
ZIP   /MB:     0 zipped,     0   saved
MEMCTL/MB:     0   curr,     0 target, 83813 max

   GID NAME             MEMSZ     GRANT    SZTGT      TCHD    TCHD W MCTL?   MCTLSZ   MCTLTGT  MCT
32095121 scpro3 (763bc33 131072.00 131060.00 131656.54  2621.44  2621.44   Y     0.00    0.00 8
32095123 vm-vmx.18155303 131072.00 131060.00 131656.54  2621.44  2621.44   Y     0.00    0.00 8
32095124 vm-vmm.18155303 131072.00 131060.00 131656.54  2621.44  2621.44   Y     0.00    0.00 8
20065505 hostd.11353859      77.73    60.34    66.38    21.08    21.08   N     0.00    0.00
20067162 sfcb-ProviderMa     56.10    53.41    56.10    36.92    36.92   N     0.00    0.00
20067153 sfcb-ProviderMa     31.68    21.62    23.78     7.18     7.18   N     0.00    0.00
20066143 vpxa.11354279       25.31    17.47    19.22     3.72     3.72   N     0.00    0.00
20066953 fdm.11354803        18.19    12.71    13.98     2.24     2.24   N     0.00    0.00
20067151 sfcb-ProviderMa     17.87    15.12    16.63     2.64     2.64   N     0.00    0.00
20066069 vobd.11354219       12.29     1.38     1.52     1.27     1.27   N     0.00    0.00
20065321 rhttpproxy.1135     10.91     6.04     6.64     1.08     1.08   N     0.00    0.00
    832 vmsyslogd.8666        7.62     5.34     5.88     5.24     5.24   N     0.00    0.00
20067168 sfcb-ProviderMa      6.34     1.86     2.04     0.32     0.32   N     0.00    0.00
   3115 dcui.9902             6.33     1.69     1.86     1.24     1.24   N     0.00    0.00
    898 vmkeventd.8717        6.00     1.80     1.98     1.79     1.79   N     0.00    0.00
20065917 smartd.11354075      5.93     2.92     3.21     0.60     0.60   N     0.00    0.00
    830 vmsyslogd.8665        5.30     4.17     4.58     3.91     3.91   N     0.00    0.00
43633273 esxtop.24684752      5.15     2.10     2.31     1.12     1.12   N     0.00    0.00
20065391 storageRM.11353      5.00     1.43     1.57     0.12     0.12   N     0.00    0.00
   1122 vmkdevmgr.8846        4.37     1.31     1.44     1.09     1.09   N     0.00    0.00
20065251 net-lbt.1135372      4.16     1.25     1.37     0.35     0.35   N     0.00    0.00
20065993 dcbd.11354179        4.09     1.08     1.19     0.05     0.05   N     0.00    0.00
20066963 sfcb-ProviderMa      3.76     2.21     2.43     1.63     1.63   N     0.00    0.00
20065181 vmware-usbarbit      2.94     0.35     0.39     0.19     0.19   N     0.00    0.00
20065747 net-lacp.113539      2.49     0.73     0.80     0.03     0.03   N     0.00    0.00
    336 init.8433             2.24     0.09     0.09     0.07     0.07   N     0.00    0.00
   3111 sh.9900               2.24     0.09     0.09     0.07     0.07   N     0.00    0.00
20067139 sfcb-ProviderMa      2.04     0.41     0.45     0.27     0.27   N     0.00    0.00
20065027 ntpd.11353577        1.76     0.38     0.41     0.21     0.21   N     0.00    0.00
```

Figure 2.7

Table – 2.3 Important Memory Metrics

Memory Metrics	Description
MEM overcommit avg	The MEM overcommit avg metrics show the average physical memory overcommitment. A value of 0.15 shows a 15 percent overcommitment and 0.40 shows an overcommitment of 40 percent.
PMEM	The **total** field shows the total amount of the vSphere host's memory and the vmk field shows the amount of memory used by VMkernel. The **other** field shows the amount of memory that is used by everything else except the VMkernel. The **free** field shows the memory that is not being used.
VMKMEM	This shows more statistics of VMkernel memory. The **Min Free** field shows the amount of memory VMkernel keeps free. The **rsvd** field shows the reserved physical memory for resource pools. The **unrsvd** field shows the amount of unreserved memory.

Memory Metrics	Description
PSHARE	PSHARE shows the stats about TPS, and it has three fields: shared, common, and saving about page-sharing information. The **shared** field shows the amount of physical memory shared among virtual machines or resources. The **common** field shows the amount of memory that is common for all the resources. Finally, the **saving** field shows the amount of memory that is being saved by TPS.
SWAP	This shows the total memory swapped out for all resources. The **curr** field shows the current swap usage and the **rclmtgt** field shows the memory that can be reclaimed by a vSphere host.
ZIP	The **zipped** field shows the total compressed physical memory and the **saved** field shows the saved compressed memory.
MEMCTL	This shows the memory ballooning information.

Virtual machine related memory metrics

Memory Metrics	Description
MCTL	The MCTL field shows if the balloon driver has been installed or not.
MEMSZ	This shows the amount of memory allocated to a virtual machine.
SWTGT	This presents the amount of swap space the host predicts a virtual machine would use.
MCTLSZ	If the value of this field is greater than zero, the vSphere host makes virtual machines expand their balloon driver. The threshold value of this field is 1.
SWCUR	This field shows the amount of swap space used by a virtual machine. A value > 0 shows the host has already swapped memory pages. The threshold value is 1.
SWR/s	When SWR/s is greater than zero, it means the vSphere host system is swapping memory pages in from the hard disk. The threshold value is 1, and that indicates excessive memory overcommitment.
SWW/s	When SWW/s is greater than zero, it means the vSphere host system is swapping memory out to the hard disk. The threshold value for this field is 1, and this also indicates excessive memory overcommitment.
SWPWT	This field shows the percentage of waiting time for memory to be swapped in from the disk for a virtual machine. The threshold value for this field is 5.

Memory Metrics	Description
CACHEUSD	If the value of this field is greater than zero, the vSphere host system has compressed memory. The threshold value of this field is 0, and this indicates excessive memory overcommitment.
Zip	The threshold value for this field is zero. If its value gets greater than zero the vSphere host system is actively compressing the memory and indicates memory over commitment.
Unzip	The threshold value for this field is zero. If its value is greater than zero, then the vSphere host system will be the active memory to decompress it.

Diagnosing memory blockage

The following four host free memory stats are very important when it comes to diagnosing memory bottleneck and memory overcommitment: hard, low, high, and soft, represented by four thresholds. The threshold values for these metrics depend on how much physical memory a vSphere host has.

The threshold value for `highstate` is represented by `minfree`. You can see this in the following screenshot. VMkernel keeps some amount of memory free, which is shown by `minfree`.

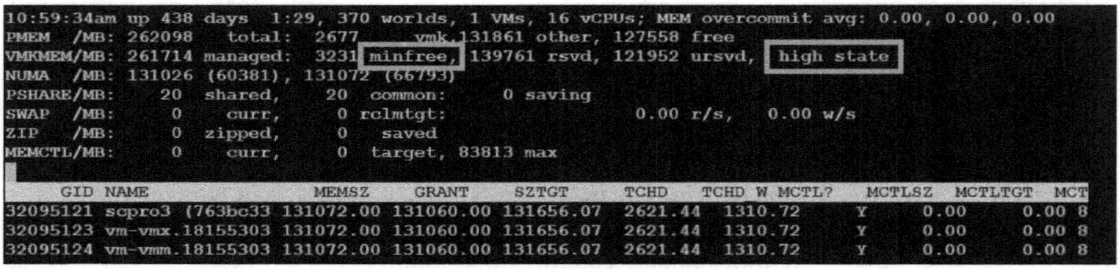

Figure 2.8

As page-sharing is enabled in the vSphere host system by default, it manages to reclaim memory with a very small overhead. It tries to determine from `highstate` when to reclaim physical memory using swapping or ballooning. A vSphere host system will try to reclaim memory that has already been allocated to virtual machines once it gets low on memory resources. When a vSphere system gets low on memory, the aforementioned metrics can be examined to determine if the vSphere host system is trying to reclaim memory.

As highlighted in *Figure 2.8*, the vSphere host is reporting `highstate`. That means the vSphere host does not presently have memory contention. If this changes into `softstate`, it means a vSphere host will use ballooning to reclaim memory. If this changes into `hardstate`, then a vSphere host will use compression and swapping to reclaim memory. Finally, if the vSphere host shows `lowstate`, all memory reclamation methods (ballooning, compression, swapping) are used together to reclaim memory.

Your host should not be swapping memory, as that can have a negative effect on the virtual machines and the vSphere host's performance itself. This can be monitored from the vCenter performance charts that I will cover later in the chapter. The preceding values should be as low as possible on a healthy vSphere host system. Whenever you see a vSphere host reporting `softstate`, it indicates that the host is having a memory contention problem. The ballooning can be viewed by enabling the `MTCL` and `MCTLSZ` metrics. As mentioned in the previous topic, *Esxtop for memory statistics*, enable the *j* field to view `MCTL?` and `MCTLSZ`. This observation can save you a lot of time if your vSphere host system's memory is in good shape or if it's time for a memory upgrade.

A lot of memory swapping is also not good for a vSphere host. If a vSphere host keeps swapping memory actively, it will have a bad impact and result upon the virtual machine's performance degradation. You can observe this by monitoring the `%SWPWT` field to see if a virtual machine is being affected by swapping. This field is not in the memory screen but can be found in the CPU screen. As I have explained earlier, `%SWPWT` shows the percentage of swap waiting time for a virtual machine to swap its pages in the memory.

GID	NAME	NWLD	%USED	%RUN	%SYS	%WAIT	%VMWAIT	%RDY	%IDLE	%OVRLP	%CSTP	%MLMTD	%SWPWT
1	idle	32	1969.18	3200.00	0.00	0.00		3200.00	0.00	1.05	0.00	0.00	0.00
32095121	scpro3 (763bc33	24	3.57	5.73	0.17	2400.00	0.00	0.43	1975.74	0.05	0.00	0.00	3.57
43845691	esxtop.24444318	1	2.58	4.29	0.00	100.00	-	0.00	0.00	0.00	0.00	0.00	0.00
20065505	hostd.11353859	25	0.27	0.45	0.00	2500.00	-	0.07	0.00	0.00	0.00	0.00	0.00
20066143	vpxa.11354279	19	0.23	0.38	0.00	1900.00	-	0.06	0.00	0.00	0.00	0.00	0.00
20065251	net-lbt.1135372	1	0.17	0.28	0.00	100.00	-	0.00	0.00	0.00	0.00	0.00	0.00
2	system	10	0.13	0.22	0.01	1000.00	-	0.02	0.00	0.00	0.00	0.00	0.00
20066953	fdm.11354803	18	0.13	0.21	0.01	1800.00	-	0.06	0.00	0.00	0.00	0.00	0.00
8	helper	90	0.10	0.18	0.00	9000.00	-	0.06	0.00	0.01	0.00	0.00	0.00
20065321	rhttpproxy.1135	11	0.06	0.09	0.00	1100.00	-	0.05	0.00	0.00	0.00	0.00	0.00

Figure 2.9

You can see in the preceding figure that the `%SWPWT` is `3.57`. This represents the percentage swap waiting time for the virtual machine to wait for its memory pages to be swapped. This will affect the virtual machine's performance. The threshold value of this field is 5, but any value above zero is not ideal for the performance of virtual machines. If this reaches to 5, the cause needs to be inspected minutely.

You can troubleshoot this by examining why memory is overcommitting and if its allocation among virtual machines is according to available memory resources. You should also check if the memory ballooning drivers are correctly installed and present in the virtual machines to ensure ballooning is being used for swapping instead of hard swapping. You should always install VMtools on the virtual machines to ensure the installation of ballooning drivers. The MCTL? column (*Figure 2.3*) can be used to examine if the ballooning driver is installed. In *Figure 2.3*, N in MCTL? indicates that the ballooning driver is not installed on the virtual machine. The value Y in the MCTL? column indicates that the ballooning driver is installed in the virtual machine. The MCTLSZ column shows how much of the balloon is inflated within the virtual machine. If the value is 200 MB in the MCTLSZ column, that means the balloon driver is able to reclaim 200 MB of memory.

> The minfree can be tuned with the mem.memfreepct advanced setting.

Network metrics

The third common type of metrics that can be obtained from esxtop is network metrics. These metrics can help you troubleshoot network usage for your vSphere host and the virtual machines:

1. Connect to a vSphere host using SSH and log in as root or an administrative user.

2. In the command prompt, type esxtop without any flags.

3. Press *n* to view the network screen. This screen displays detailed information about network usage.

4. You need to enable some additional information for the physical network properties of vSphere hosts in esxtop for the **UP** (uplink), **FULLDUPLEX**, **SPEED, TEAM-PNIC** fields. Press *c* to enable the aforementioned fields; you can press *c* again to remove any field.

5. Press *f* to go into the **Current Field Order** screen.

6. Press the *Esc* key to return to the esxtop network statistics screen.

Understanding network metrics

In esxtop, network statistics are displayed for each port of a virtual switch. These ports are then either linked as uplinks to a physical network adapter or they are connected to a virtual network adapter of a virtual machine. When a port is utilized by a virtual machine, a world ID of that machine and its name is shown in the **USED-BY** field. You can use the world ID to distinguish the VM group. You will not see a world ID in this field if VMKernel is using the port as displayed in *Figure 2.10* (vmk0, vmk1, vmk2). The vmk network adapters can be created as required for VMotion. The last type of port is the **Management** port, which is internally used for the management of vSwitch. You can also identify the uplink ports by examining the **UP** field. The value **Y** is displayed in the **UP** field against the ports that are uplinks. The **TEAM-PNIC** field shows the name of the uplink used for the team uplink.

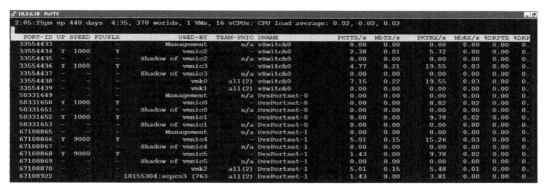

Figure 2.10

Table 2.4 Some common Network Metrics and their description

Network Metrics	Description
PORT - ID	This shows the ports IDs for the vSphere host's virtual switch.
DNAME	This shows the name of the virtual switch.
SPEED	The SPEED metric is associated with the properties of physical NICs. It shows the speed of a link in megabits per second. The preceding figure shows **four** uplinks with the speed of 1 GBs and two uplinks with the spead of 10 GBs.
FDUPLX	The FDUPLX metric is also associated with the properties of physical NICs. If this field shows Y, the physical network link is operated in full duplex mode; N indicates otherwise.
PKTTX/s	This field shows the number of packets sent per second.
MbTX/s	This shows the number of megabits sent per second.
PKTRX/s	This shows the number of packets received per second.

Network Metrics	Description
MbRX/s	This shows the number of megabits received per second.
%DRPTX	This field shows the percentage of dropped sent packets.
%DRP	This field shows the percentage of dropped received packets.

Diagnosing network performance

A good starting point for diagnosing network performance can be the percentage of dropped packets. The percentage of transmitted drop packets can imply that the destination that is receiving packets is busy at that time or the transmitted network is too occupied for sending the packets on time.

Let's understand how a virtual machine transmits traffic across the wire. First, a virtual machine tries to buffer the traffic that needs to be transmitted. Once the buffer is ready to be processed, the traffic is sent to the vSwitch queue. Whenever the vSwitch queue becomes full, the rest of the packets are discarded. You can observe this in the last two columns: %DRPTX and %DRPRX. There can be two different reasons for these packets being dropped. A virtual machine with inaccurate network drivers can cause this problem. High CPU utilization by a virtual machine can also cause packet dropping.

Sometimes, insufficient capacity of an uplink that couldn't handle the requirement of network traffic for the virtual machines could also cause dropping of network packets. This issue can be resolved by distributing your virtual machines to other hosts in your cluster. For this reason, you should always stick to vSphere network design best practices to avoid bottlenecks in production.

Storage metrics

Before we start exploring disk performance metrics, I will walk you through three different screens for the disk metrics. The first storage metrics screen is called disk device view, where you can view LUN information; the second one is the disk VM screen where you can see the statistics per virtual machine basis; and the last one is the disk adapter screen where you can view the information of disk statistics per **host bus adapter (HBA)** basis.

Let's access esxtop to view the disk statistics in the LUN mode:

1. Connect to a vSphere host using SSH and log in as root or an administrative user.
2. In the command prompt, type esxtop without any flags.

3. Press *u* to switch **disk device** screen. This screen displays detailed information about storage, including your LUN, available data stores, shares, and number of objects.

4. Press *f* to go into **Current Field Order** screen.

5. You need to enable some additional information for the **Number of Objects** and **Shares** fields. Press *c* and then press *d* to enable the preceding fields.

6. Press the *Esc* key to return to the esxtop **disk statistics** screen.

7. Press *s* and enter 2 to set the refresh time to every 2 seconds. It will bring to you the following screen:

Figure 2.11

Storage Metrics	Description
CMDS/s	This field shows the total quantity of commands (metadata) per second. The commands include **Input/Output Operations Per Second**, SCSCI commands, disk locks, among others. The commands either come from the storage device or from the virtual machine.
DAVG/cmd	This refers to Device Average Latency, and the field shows the average time a command takes to respond to a device in milliseconds. That could be a host bus adapter or a storage device.
KAVG/cmd	The refers to Kernel Average Latency, and the field shows the amount of time an I/O request remains waiting inside the vSphere storage stack or in VMkernel. The threshold for this field is 2.

Storage Metrics	Description
QAVG/cmd	This refers to Queue Average Latency, and it presents the time consumed remaining in a queue inside the vSphere Storage Stack.
GAVG/cmd	This refers to **Guest Average Latency (GAVG)**, and it presents the response time as seen by the guest operating system. GAVG can be calculated by adding **Kernel Average Latency (KAVG)** and **Device Average Latency (DAVG)**.
READS/s	This refers to the number of Read commands per second.
WRITES/s	This is the number of Write commands per second.
MBREAD/s	This reads in megabytes per second.
MBWRTN/s	This writes in megabytes per second.
QUED	This field specifies the number of commands currently queued in VMkernel.
ABRTS/s	This field specifies the number of commands aborted per second
RESETS/s	This field specifies the number of commands reset per second.
CONS/s	This shows the SCSI Reservation Conflicts per seconds. A lot of conflicts can cause performance degradation, and they occur because of VMFS. The threshold value for this is 20.

For your application workloads, I/O latency from 20 milliseconds to 25 milliseconds can result in performance degradation. Though this is not a hard and fast rule for I/O intensive applications these values can significantly differ. For example, one application can be very IO intensive while the other application may not be as such. As I have stated in the preceding table, GAVG is a total of two latencies: DAVG and KAVG. Ideally, KAVG should be as miming as possible: the best value to achieve is zero, and the threshold value can be considered as 2 milliseconds. In addition to this, GAVG and DAVG should not be increased more than 25 milliseconds, or your system will have some I/O performance issues and the problem will need to be investigated further. You can start investigating from the storage metrics and expand the investigation to your SAN, LUNs, and storage switches.

Downloading the example code

You can download the example code files from your account at http://www.packtpub.com for all the Packt Publishing books you have purchased. If you purchased this book elsewhere, you can visit http://www.packtpub.com/support and register to have the files e-mailed directly to you.

Using vMA and resxtop

As part of vCli, rsxtop is a remote version of esxtop that comes up with the vMA appliance. Rsxtop can also be used in three operational modes: interactive, batch, and replay modes. Perform the following instructions to use resxtop from VMWare vMA appliance to examine the network matrices:

1. Log in to vMA as vi-admin.

2. Add a server as a vMA target by running the following command:

   `vifp addserver crimv3esx002.linxsol.com --authpolicy fpauth`

3. Now set it as the target server to perform operations:

   `vifptarget --set crimv3esx002.linxsol.com`

4. Once the target is set, simply type the following command in the console: `resxtop`.

5. This will take you to the esxtop interactive command, where you can follow the procedures described to interact with different vSphere host performance metrics.

6. Once you are done, type the following command in the console to remove the target server from vMA:

   `vifpremove removeserver crimv3esx002.linxsol.com`

```
vi-admin@vma:~> vifp addserver crimv3esx002.linxsol.com --authpolicy fpauth
root@crimv3esx002.linxsol.com's password:
vi-admin@vma:~> vifpvtarget --set crimv3esx002.linxsol.com
vi-admin@vma:~ [crimv3esx002.linxsol.com]> resxtop
```

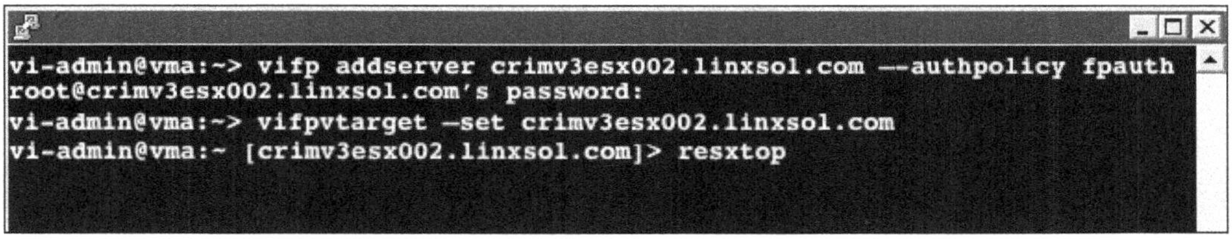

Figure 2.12

vCenter performance charts

VMware provides another great tool to monitor and troubleshoot vSphere host performance using its charts. These charts can be very helpful and offer user-friendly ways to diagnose vSphere host problems. You can easily create new charts, customize metrics, customize the time, and save the settings. Alternatively, VMware has provided built-in general purpose options for the charts to use the existing settings. The chart does not only offer real-time monitoring but also presents information about the past day, week, month, or year. In this section, we will go through the following topics briefly:

- Creating charts
- Configuring metrics
- Configuring logging level for performance

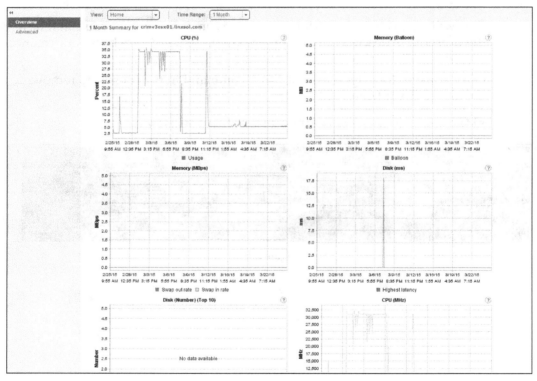

Figure 2.13

You can choose two options when viewing the charts: **Overview** and **Advanced**. As you can see in the preceding figure, both options can be found in the left column. You can find some of the most common preconfigured metrics in the **Overview** chart, for example CPU usage, memory ballooning, memory, disk usage/latency, and network usage. In **Advanced** charts, you can see the real-time metrics of CPU, memory, network, or storage, as seen in the following screenshot:

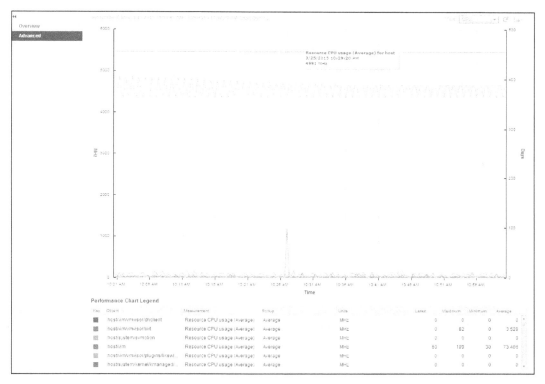

Figure 2.14

Creating a chart and configuring metrics

As you have already seen the important metrics in previous sections, it will be easy for you to quickly select which metric you need to view when you are troubleshooting. For example, if you are facing slow disk performance in vSphere, you would like to choose the **Highest Latency**, **Read Latency**, and **Write Latency** metrics to perform a quick performance check. Following are the steps to create a chart and configure different metrics accordingly.

1. Log in to your vSphere web client.

2. Click on vCenter in the left pane.

3. Click on **Hosts and Clusters** in the left pane.

4. Click on **Datacenter** and then cluster to expand the view so that you can see the hosts.

5. Click on a host that you would like to monitor the performance of. It will take you to the new windows.

6. From the right pane, click on the **Monitor** tab, and under this tab, click on the **Performance** tab. Now you can see the **Overview** chart with the default metrics. Click on **Advanced** to go to the advanced charts view.

7. Click on **Chart Options** at top. This will present the **Chart Options** window as seen in the following figure:

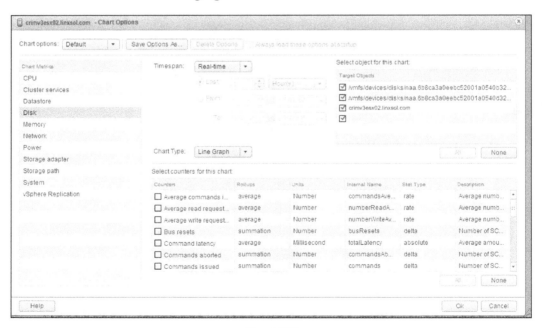

Figure 2.15

8. Select **Disk** from the left pane. Scroll down to select the **High Latency** counter from the **Counters** list at the bottom. You can also choose the **Graph** type from the **Chart Type**.

9. Now click on **Save Options As**, save it with the name Disk Metrics, and click **OK**.

10. It will load your new chart, as you can see in the following screenshot—the highest disk latency you can see in this screenshot is 2 Millisecond.

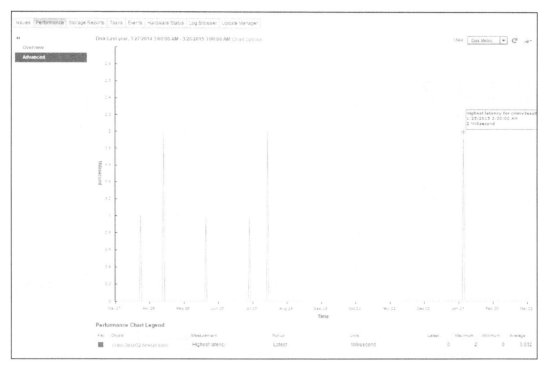

Figure 2.16

11. If you want to export this chart, you can export it to JPEG, PNG, and CSV formats by clicking this icon on your chart:

Figure 2.17

12. You can delete the chart by clicking on **Chart Options**. Make sure that the selected chart is **Disk Metric** and then click on **Delete Options** to delete the chart.

 For detailed information about charts, visit: `https://pubs.` `vmware.com/vsphere-55/topic/com.vmware.ICbase/` `PDF/vsphere-esxi-vcenter-server-55-monitoring-` `performance-guide.pdf.`

Configuring logging level for performance

The VMware vCenter Server provides you with the option of configuring statistics intervals for how often data should be captured, how long the data should remain in the database, and what kind data it should be collecting.

1. Log in to your vSphere client and click on **vCenter Server Settings**. This will open up a new window.

2. Click on **Statistics** in the left column.

3. From here, you can choose the **Interval Duration** of the metrics, how long the vCenter Server should store the data of these metrics, and at what level these statistics should be collected.

4. Click the first interval **5 Minutes** and then click **Edit**. A new window will pop up.

5. You can configure **Statistics Level** from 1 to 4 in this window. The higher the statistics level, the more data it will collect with more counters. **Level 4** will collect data for all the counters supported by the vCenter Server. For now, you can choose **Level 2** and click **OK**.

6. Click **OK** again to exit the **Statistics** window.

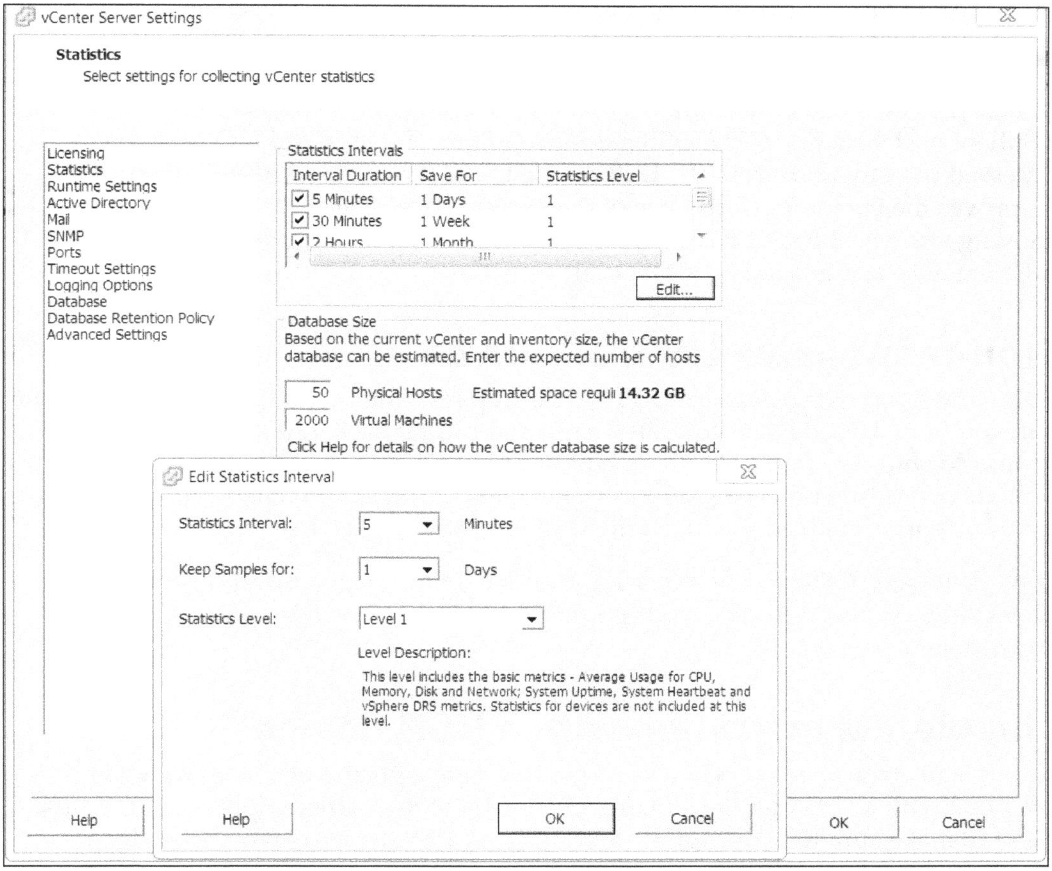

Figure 2.18

Virtual machine troubleshooting

You can face some common problems with your virtual machine's life cycle in a vSphere infrastructure. I will cover some of the potential problems and how to troubleshoot them in the following sections:

- USB-attached virtual machines
- Fault-tolerant virtual machines

USB-attached virtual machines

In the recent versions of ESXi (4.0 and later), a USB device can be controlled by a virtual machine autonomously, and the virtual machine is fully responsible for managing it using VMDirectPath. Using VMDirectPath, a USB drive remains attached to the virtual machine while the virtual machine is transferred to other vSphere host systems. In the USB pass-through mechanism, the I/O requests can be accessed directly to or from the USB device to the virtual machines. This not only improves the overall performance of the vSphere host system but also benefits us moving and attaching USB devices to different virtual machines using vMotion and a USB device is managed by VMkernel.

Non-responsive USB/CD drives

Sometimes your CD drive and USB device stop responding and remains in that state forever. For a USB device, you can detach and plug it back. If it still doesn't work, then cold shut down your vSphere host system for a minute or so and remove the USB device before powering on the system again. You should check in BIOS if the USB support is enabled. Reattach the USB drive and try again.

If while using a CD drive or accessing it an ISO image gets nonresponsive at the client side, you need to close your vSphere client and open it up again to resolve the problem.

Unable VM migration with a USB device

You see an error message when you try to migrate a virtual machine, which is attached with a USB device from one vSphere host to another vSphere host. You need to make sure the appropriate and updated USB device drivers are installed on the virtual machine. This problem can occur because of unavailability of vMotion for the USB device. You need to ensure that vMotion is enabled for the USB device in the USB device settings. Another cause could be that your vSphere host system does not support vMotion with a USB device or a disable VMkernel port for vMotion to allow USB traffic.

 You can find a list of approved USB devices in the VMware Knowledge Base KB1021345. The list is updated regularly.

Fault-tolerant virtual machines

In an ideal virtualization environment, you would like to minimize failover rates and increase its performance as much as possible. I will cover some of the most common errors to give you a flavor of troubleshooting Fault Tolerance errors of virtual machines. It is not possible to cover all the errors in this book, but you can always consult VMware Knowledge Base.

Incompatible or hosts not available

Sometimes, you try to power on a virtual machine and you receive an error of unavailability of a compatible host in your cluster, although you may have hosts with enough available resources in your cluster to accommodate virtual machines. The possible causes for this can be that you do not have a datastore attached with your hosts or that hardware virtualization is not enabled. You need to confirm that the datastores are correctly connected with the host; you also need to ensure that hardware virtualization is enabled on your hosts.

Summary

In this chapter, we saw how to use performance-monitoring tools and how these tools can help us to troubleshoot some very common issues in a vSphere infrastructure. We also went through some of the very important vSphere host metrics and discovered how these metrics can be viewed in Performance Charts.

In the next chapter, we will dive into troubleshooting vSphere clusters. We will discuss how we can monitor the performance of these clusters. What are the common DRS-enabled storage problems and how to troubleshoot such problems? How to determine, and what should we do, if we have insufficient resources? We will also look into some of the vSphere fault-tolerance problems, and finally, take a look at how to configure SNMP traps for vSphere infrastructure monitoring.

Troubleshooting Clusters

3

Today's virtual environment is not considered complete until it remains online 24/7. High availability is supported by almost all kinds of operating systems, regardless of its type. VMware also supports high availability and the **Distributed Resource Scheduler** (**DRS**) to allow you to have a fully automated and highly available infrastructure. DRS manages the workload and load balances them within the vSphere cluster. It is based on advanced algorithms to automate the migration of virtual machines using vMotion from one host to another when the resources are not available to satisfy the virtual machine requirements on a particular host. The migrations are done entirely without any downtime.

To avoid downtime and to monitor the performance of your infrastructure, you must know how to troubleshoot DRS and high availability issues in VMware infrastructure. In this chapter, you will also see how to troubleshoot vMotion and storage vMotion issues. You have already seen in *Chapter 1*, *The Methodology of Problem Solving*, how important business continuity is in the 24/7 highly available environment and what it means for a seasonal system administrator of the infrastructure.

In this chapter, we will cover the following topics:

- Overview of cluster information
- Cluster performance monitoring
- Failing heartbeat datastore
- DRS-enabled storage
- Insufficient resource troubleshooting
- I/O control troubleshooting
- vSphere fault tolerance
- Configuring SNMP traps for continuous monitoring

An overview of cluster information

Let's start by looking into the cluster information from the vSphere web client:

1. Log in to your vSphere web client.

2. Click on **vCenter** in the left pane.

3. Now click on **Hosts and Clusters** from the inventory tree.

4. Click on the arrow of data center to view all the children under it.

5. Click on the cluster, and then click on the **Summary** tab on the right under **Actions**.

6. You can see a vSphere cluster named **LinxSol-FatNodes** in the following screenshot:

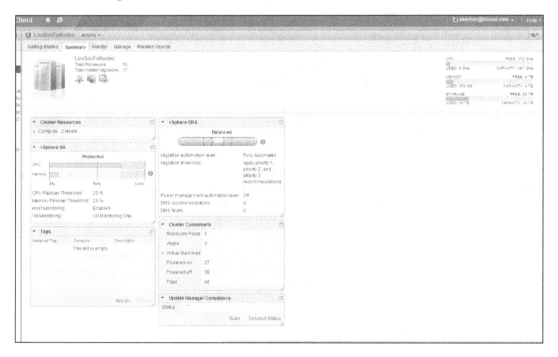

You can see a summary of information about the vSphere cluster named LinxSol-FatNodes. The top column shows the total number of processors and the total number of vMotion migrations. In the same pane, you can see on the right the total **CPU**, **MEMORY**, **STORAGE** and their usage respectively. The **Cluster Resources** pane shows the number of hosts the cluster is made up of, total processors, CPU resources in GHz, total memory, and the EVC mode.

The **vSphere HA** pane shows information about vSphere HA protection status, percentage of **CPU Failover Threshold**, percentage of **Memory Failover Threshold**, status of **Host Monitoring**, and status of **VM Monitoring**. You can monitor a brief summary of your vSphere DRS from the vSphere DRS column. This column provides you with information about **Migration automation level**, whether it is **Manual, Partially automated**, or **Fully automated**. As you can see, in my case it is **Fully automated**, and DRS has automatically decided to place and migrate virtual machines to optimize resources. It also shows information about the **Migration threshold, Power management automation level**, number of **DRS recommendations**, and number of **DRS faults**. The next pane **Cluster Consumers** shows information about consumer resources that are utilizing the resources of the cluster. It includes the information about the number of **Resource Pools**, number of **vApps**, and number of **Virtual Machines**.

Cluster performance monitoring

You have already seen how to monitor the performance of vSphere hosts using charts. The vSphere web client also provides you charts to monitor the performance of a vSphere cluster. You have also learned the counters in these charts as covered in the previous chapter, so I will briefly summarize it. Follow these steps to monitor vSphere cluster performance:

1. Log in to your vSphere web client.

2. Click on **vCenter** in the left pane.

3. Now click on **Hosts and Clusters** from the inventory tree.

4. Click on the arrow of data center to view all the children under it.

5. Click on the cluster, and then click on the **Monitor** tab on the right under **Actions**.

6. Now click on the **Performance** tab under **Monitor**.

7. You will see a vSphere chart **Overview** for cluster named **LinxSol-FatNodes** with two charts, one for **CPU** and one for **Memory** measured in MHz and MB respectively, as seen in the following screenshot. By default, it will show you one-day usage summary of both CPU and Memory.

8. From the **View** dropdown menu, you can choose **Home** (selected by default), **Resource Pools & Virtual Machines**, and **Hosts**. You can select any of the three to monitor their CPU and Memory usage.

9. From the **Time Range** dropdown menu, you can choose a period of time, from one day to a year or a custom range:

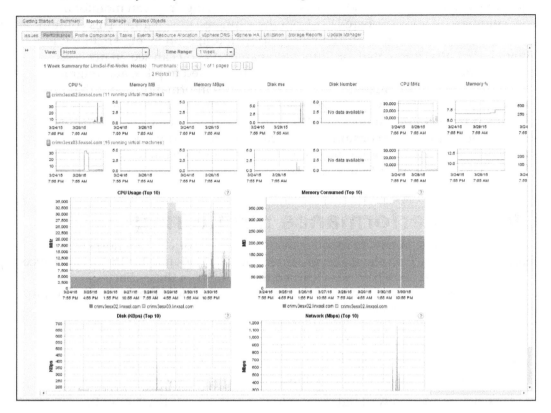

You can see in the preceding screenshot a cluster comprising two vSphere hosts and their collected metrics for a duration of the last thirty days.

vSphere HA

VMware vSphere HA protects virtual machines and vSphere hosts in a cluster by providing high availability. The vSphere HA agent monitors vSphere hosts and detects any failure occurring in the hosts. Once a vSphere host fails, vSphere HA restarts virtual machines to another available vSphere host. In a vSphere cluster, a host is elected as a master host by the vSphere HA agent and other hosts are elected as slaves. The master host monitors the slave hosts in the cluster and also monitors state of the virtual machines that are being protected by vSphere HA. The vSphere HA agent is installed on the vSphere host when it is added to a vSphere cluster.

The agent then communicates with the other vSphere agents that it finds in the cluster. A vSphere cluster can have a single vSphere host as a master, and the remaining vSphere hosts are slave hosts. If a vSphere master host fails, a reelection is held and a new master host is elected.

Failing heartbeat datastores

What do humans usually do if they find an irregular or missing heartbeat? They consult with the doctor to cure it. When a vSphere cluster misses a heartbeat, you are required to troubleshoot it before it leads to the disaster of a failing cluster.

A vSphere host's HA management traffic is usually separated from other networks by using a dedicated management network. In a vSphere cluster, the master vSphere host uses the management network to interconnect with a slave vSphere host. The datastore heartbeat is used when a slave vSphere host fails to respond to the calls of its master host. The master host tries to establish communication using a datastore network partition and tries to find the slave host's heart beating in it. When a master vSphere host is unable to find the slave host's heart beating, it declares it to be in a failed state. Then, the master vSphere host tries to find other available slave host that can host the virtual machines of the failed slave host. The master host determines the slave hosts with available resources and then restarts all the virtual machines of the failed slave host to other slave hosts.

Changing heartbeating datastores

You will learn how to configure a heartbeat datastore of your choice in the following context. By default, vCenter Server allocates different sets of datastores. The datastores are selected by vCenter Server to maximize access to a single datastore by vSphere hosts. vCenter Server also ensures that the heartbeat datastores are not hosted on the same NFS server or do not belong the same storage pool. Perform the following steps to examine the vSphere HA settings in a vSphere web client:

1. Connect with your vCenter Server using the web client. From the vSphere web client, click on the vCenter Server to get into vCenter Server menu.

2. Click on **Hosts and Clusters** in the left column. This will take you to the **Hosts and Clusters** menu.

3. From the left column menu, expand **Data Center** and then click on a cluster you want to change the heartbeating datastores.

4. In the right-hand side column, click on the **Manage** tab and then on the **Settings** tab under it.

5. In the **Settings** tab, select vSphere HA from the **Services** menu on the left. It will take you to the vSphere HA settings column.

6. In the vSphere HA menu, you can expand **Datastore Heartbeating** to view the currently selected datastores.

7. Click on the **Edit** button on the right side of this column and a pop-up box will come up.

8. Click on **Datastore Heartbeating** to expand it.

9. To choose a specific datastore, select the second option: **Use datastores only from the specific list**.

10. Select the datastore by clicking on the checkbox before the datastore name you want for heartbeats.

11. Click **OK** to close the settings.

Insufficient heartbeat datastores

Sometimes you can face an error complaint about insufficient heartbeat datastores. The following error comes up when there is only one datastore available:

 The number of vSphere HA heartbeat datastores for this host is 1 which is less than required 2.

Ideally, you should add an additional datastore to prevent this error. But you can also suppress the error by tuning the host configuration alarm. You can tune the advanced settings of `das.ignoreInsufficientHBDatastore` to `true`, which is configured as `false` by default.

1. Log in to your vCenter Server using the web client.
2. Click on **Hosts and Clusters** in the left-hand side column.
3. From the left column menu, expand **Data Center** and then click on a cluster you want to change the heart beating datastores.
4. In the right-hand side column, click on the **Manage** tab and then on the **Settings** tab under it.
5. In the **Settings** tab, select vSphere HA from the **Services** menu on the left-hand side. It will take you to the **vSphere HA Settings** column.
6. Click on the **Edit** button on the right-hand side of this column, and a pop-up box will appear.
7. Click on **Advanced Options** and then on the **Add** button.
8. In the **Option** column, insert the following line, and in the **Value** column, insert **true**:

   das.ignoreInsufficientHBDatastore

9. Click **OK** to close the **Advanced Options**.
10. Right-click on the vSphere host that is displaying the alarm and choose **Reconfigure for vSphere HA**.

Unable to unmount a datastore

You can face the following error sometimes while unmounting a datastore: The HA agent on host 'crimv3esx009.linxsol.com' failed to quiesce file activity on datastore 'NFS001'.

This problem normally appears when the vSphere heartbeat files remain open in the network partition and are not closed. Essentially, vCenter Server eliminates a datastore from the heartbeats and elects a new one when you try to unmount a datastore that is being used by other heartbeats. The HA agent is not notified about the new datastores with heartbeats when a host is isolated and the network partition is not reachable. Datastores are not accessible sometimes when the storage fails, and if you are using multiple paths to reach your storage, all of the paths become inaccessible.

> To unmount a datastore from **Storage Datastore Cluster**, first decommission it by dragging it out of the storage cluster. You can then right-click on the datastore in the vSphere client and click on **Unmount** to unmount the datastore.

Detaching datastores with vMA

Once you have a decommissioned datastore, it could be a little hectic to detach it from all the hosts manually. What if you have fifty vSphere hosts and you need to detach it one by one from all the hosts. You can use the **VMware Management Assistant (vMA)** to automate detachment. Now we will use it to delete a datastore. If you need help or further explanation about vSphere vMA appliance, please refer to *Chapter 1, The Methodology of Problem Solving*.

1. Log in to the vSphere vMA appliance through SSH as a vi-admin user.

2. Add a server as a vMA target by running the following command:

   ```
   vi-admin@vma:~> vifp addserver crimv3esx003.linxsol.com
   --authpolicy fpauth --username root
   ```

3. Now, set it as the target server to execute storage operations:

   ```
   vi-admin@vma:~> vifptarget --set crimv3esx003.linxsol.com
   ```

4. Next, use the `vicfg-nas` command to list all available datastores to the host:

   ```
   vi-admin@vma:~[crimv3esx003.linxsol.com]> vicfg-nas -l
   ```

5. Select the name of the datastore you would like to delete. I will delete the datastore named `Heartbeat02`. Using the `-d` switch with the `vicfg-nas` command, you can delete the datastore as follows:

   ```
   vi-admin@vma:~[crimv3esx003.linxsol.com]> vicfg-nas -d Heartbeat02

   NAS volume Heartbeat02 deleted.
   ```

6. You can also use a one liner to perform the preceding operation using the vSphere vMA appliance:

```
vi-admin@vma:~ vicfg-nas -h crivm3esx003.linxsol.com -d
Heartbeat02
```

```
vi-admin@vma:~> vifp addserver crimv3esx003.linxsol.com --authpolicy fpauth --username root
root@crimv3esx003.linxsol.com's password:
vi-admin@vma:~> vifptarget --set crimv3esx003.linxsol.com
vi-admin@vma:~[crimv3esx003.linxsol.com]> vicfg-nas -l
Heartbeat1 is /heartbeat1 from nfsserver mounted
Heartbeat2 is /heartbeat2 from nfsserver mounted
NFSVol01 is /VMDK1 from nfsserver mounted
NFSVol02 is /VMDK2 from nfsserver mounted
Template is /vm_template from nfsserver mounted
vi-admin@vma:~[crimv3esx003.linxsol.com]> vicfg-nas -d Heartbeat02
NAS volume Heartbeat02 deleted.
vi-admin@vma:~[crimv3esx003.linxsol.com]> vicfg-nas -l
Heartbeat1 is /heartbeat1 from nfsserver mounted
NFSVol01 is /VMDK1 from nfsserver mounted
NFSVol02 is /VMDK2 from nfsserver mounted
Template is /vm_template from nfsserver mounted
vi-admin@vma:~[crimv3esx003.linxsol.com]>
```

7. We will use now the Perl script to automate detaching datastores from all the hosts at once. You can also use this script to mount, attach, and unmount the datastores. Download the vGhetto script from GitHub (http://goo.gl/xcz4AO) into your vSphere vMA appliance.

8. Make it executable:

```
chmod +x lunManagement.pl
```

9. Type the following options with the script to list all the datastores attached with a vCenter Server. Enter the password when prompted:

```
./lunManagment.pl -- crimv1vcs001.linxsol.com --username 'linxsol\
zeeshan' --operation list
```

10. Unmount the datastore you want to detach:

```
./lunManagement.pl -- crimv1vcs001.linxsol.com --username
'linxsol\zeeshan' --operation unmount --datastore NFSVol02
```

11. Detach NFSVol02 from all the ESXi hosts using the `lunManagement` script. Type the following in the vMA console:

```
./lunManagement.pl -- crimv1vcs001.linxsol.com --username
'linxsol\zeeshan' --operation detach --datastore NFSVol02
```

12. Confirm once it has prompted you for the password and deletion of the datastore.

Detaching a datastore using vSphere PowerCLI

You can also use vSphere PowerCLI to unmount and detach the datastore in your infrastructure with the following steps:

1. Download the community-supported script available from the VMware community at http://goo.gl/ER3OYK. Review and accept the VMware contributed sample code agreement.

2. If the script is in a text file, save it as a .ps1 file.

3. Open vSphere PowerCLI as an administrator and run the following command:

    ```
    Import-Module C:\DataStoreFunctions.ps1
    ```

4. If the preceding command complains that the script is not digitally signed in the PowerCLI shell, you can use the following command to bypass it for the current PowerCLI session:

    ```
    Set-ExecutionPolicy -Scope Process -ExectuionPolicy Bypass
    ```

5. Connect with the vCenter Server by typing the following command and replace the user name and password with your credentials:

    ```
    Connect-VIServer -Server crimv1vcs001.linxsol.com -Protocol https
    -User linxsol\zeeshan -Password yourpassword
    ```

6. Use the `Get-DatastoreMountInfo` cmdlet from the imported script to list all the datastores and their status (whether they are mounted/attached or not). Type the cmdlet in the PowerShell CLI:

    ```
    Get-DatastoreMountInfo | FT -AutoSize
    ```

7. Unmount the datastore with the following command:

```
Get-Datastore "NFSVol02" | Unmount-Datastore
```

8. The datastore is now ready to be unmounted. Now use the `Detach-Datastore` option to detach the datastore:

```
Get-Datastore "NFSVol02" | Detach-Datastore
```

The cmdlets are self-explanatory and do not require any further explanations.

vCenter server rejects specific datastores

We have seen in the previous sections how to specify particular datastores for vSphere HA storage heartbeats. But sometimes, vCenter Server doesn't accept the alternative datastores specified by you and continues using the datastores that it has already selected. In such a scenario, you should make sure to select an even number of datastores. vCenter Server automatically tries to choose the number of datastores and determines it otherwise your selection of datastores.

The number of datastores can be surpassed, as shown in the previous section, *Insufficient heartbeat datastores*, to avoid the problem. All paths are down to a datastore selected by you, which can also create such kind of problem. You always need to make sure that the datastore you want to select for a heartbeat is attached and mounted, and not in a failure state. The trickiest one in all of these errors is when a host becomes inaccessible but it doesn't stop using the existing datastore for the heartbeats. You change the heartbeat datastore from the **Datastore Heartbeating** settings, but it won't take effect. Most of the time, you can avoid getting into this by ensuring reachability among hosts and datastores and that the vSphere HA agent is also running on all the hosts normally.

DRS-enabled storage

You can automate the management of all of your datastore cluster resources using the Storage DRS. In a datastore cluster, a Storage DRS generates recommendations for migrating and placing the disks of your virtual machines to different datastores based on the availability of I/O resources and free space. DRS-enabled storage automates the load balancing of space across different datastores of a cluster. It also does the load balancing of I/O load of a virtual machine's disks and places their disks accordingly to satisfy their I/O needs.

Failed DRS recommendations

When automated, Storage DRS tries to implement the recommendations for low space or I/O load balancing; but sometimes it doesn't work and fails to apply recommendations. There could be multiple issues causing this problem that does not allow Storage DRS to apply the recommendations. You can check all the alarms that have been triggered recently. Sometimes, there is no space available in datastores to accommodate disk resources anymore. If the datastore is full, where Storage DRS decides to migrate a virtual machine, the thin provisioning threshold crossed alarm will be triggered for the target datastore and virtual machine migration will fail. In this case, you can increase and provided more space to the datastore that is running out of space or you can try to reclaim the space by removing files that are not being used anymore or have been orphaned. The space can also be reclaimed by removing snapshots. Storage DRS recommendations can also fail to be applied if the target datastore is not available, if it is entering the maintenance mode, or if it is already in the maintenance mode. In that case, you need to exit from the datastore maintenance mode, and if this fails, try to find the root cause of its failure. The failure could occur due to multiple reasons. However, make sure that network connectivity is available and vSphere hosts are able to reach to the datastores.

Storage DRS also generates multiple recommendations when you create new virtual machines or perform different day-to-day operations of cloning and relocating the existing virtual machines. Sometimes, the Storage DRS starts generating only one placement recommendation for these operations and doesn't generate alternative recommendations. Storage DRS behaves in this way when it tries to migrate a virtual machine, but a swap file has already been located in the target datastore and explicitly specified by the destination host. Storage DRS generates a single recommendation because the cluster where your disks are to be migrated do not form a single affinity group. If that happens, you can accept the recommendation generated by Storage DRS. This behavior can also be avoided by not specifying that a virtual machine's swap file location is same as the target datastore cluster.

Datastore maintenance mode failure

In the vSphere infrastructure life cycle, you often need to maintain your infrastructure. This also includes the maintenance of your datastores. However, sometimes when you try to bring a datastore into maintenance state, it takes forever to get into this state and keeps indicating remaining 1 percent in suspended state. You should check if Storage vMotion is enabled for single or multiple disks for that datastore and whether it is able to migrate the disks. You should ensure Storage DRS is not disabled on the disks. You also need to ensure if any specific Storage DRS rules have been set up, that they are not stopping Storage DRS from migrating recommendations for the disks, and that Storage DRS is enabled. If you find out it is a Storage DRS rule that is stopping a virtual machine's migration, you should disable and remove such rules.

Your vCenter Server will disable Storage DRS if it appears with the error It cannot operate on the datastore. This could happen because of a shared datastore among different datacenters and the datastore. You have Storage DRS and I/O load balancing enabled for a datastore, but you move the datastore or the host mounted with that datastore to another datacenter. The vCenter server will disable the Storage DRS and I/O load balancing for the whole datastore cluster except Storage DRS space balancing. You should move back the host or unmount the datastore, and mount it back only in one datacenter and make sure Storage I/O control is enabled for the datastore's cluster.

More common errors of Storage DRS

A very common error often faced is insufficient disk space on a datastore, which can be due to different reasons. In the Storage DRS context, you might be trying to move multiple virtual machines into a datastore cluster, but it fails after migrating one or more virtual machines successfully. When the migration process starts, Storage DRS determines the available space but is unable to determine the free space while migrating virtual machines.

Each time a migration completes successfully, it recalculates and reallocates the datastore space based on that. You should always initiate migration one by one to avoid facing this problem.

Another very common error you face often is `Operation Not Allowed in the Current State`. You attempt to create a new virtual machine or clone a virtual machine on a datastore cluster, but it fails with the aforementioned error. By default, Storage DRS enforces different rules and inspects the rule violations on a Storage DRS–enabled datastore upon creating or cloning a virtual machine.

While creating the storage disks of a new virtual machine, Storage DRS produces an error when it finds out that the disks are not being created in compliance with the Storage DRS rules. Why does Storage DRS do this? It does this because it cannot reference a virtual machine that does not exist, but is still being created. You can remove the conflicting rules and recreate the virtual machines. Sometimes, virtual hardware, for example, HD Audio Sound or other incompatible hardware, can also prevent the Storage vMotion from occurring.

Insufficient resources and vSphere HA failover

In vSphere infrastructure, we will come across many known problems in highly available clusters. In this section, we will start investigating and understanding different problems regarding insufficient resources and see how vSphere uses admission control to ensure the availability of these resources.

Here are some tips that you should follow before directly addressing the errors that will be discussed later:

- Ensure your shared storage/SAN/NAS is accessible from your vSphere hosts. You can also check the connectivity at Layer 2 and at the storage layer.

- Always verify that your vSphere networking is working normally and that you are able to reach your vCenter server, management network, gateways. Further, ensure that your vCenter server is able to reach to your vSphere hosts. I will cover this in the *Network Troubleshooting* section.

- Logs, as discussed in *Chapter 1*, *The Methodology of Problem Solving*, can be the best starting point for troubleshooting vSphere HA.

- You should always start with HA networking problems and vSphere HA agent problems.

- Always read carefully all the vSphere cluster alarms, warnings, and related events followed by the logs to get more details.

- If the HA agent on the host generates some errors or becomes unresponsive, you can attempt to use the **Reconfigure for HA** menu from the vSphere client. This will restart and reconfigure HA agent configuration on the vSphere host.

In case of host failures, vSphere HA admission control manages the reservations of these resources to restore virtual machines. In highly available infrastructures, you cannot afford HA admission control to malfunction. If it does, your virtual machines will not be recovered in case of host failures. You can see in the following screenshot for the kind of events the vSphere HA virtual machine failover failed alarm triggers:

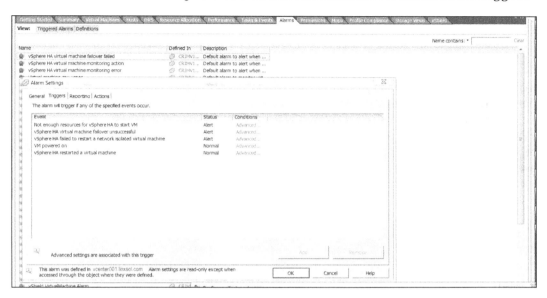

A vSphere cluster can start showing a red alarm sign in case a vSphere host is failing against the admission control policy or sufficient failover resources are not available to it. Some of the reasons for such behavior could be that the vSphere hosts forming the vSphere clusters do not have any connectivity, or a vSphere host has gone into maintenance mode and now it is not responding.

A fat virtual machine (a virtual machine with a lot of memory and CPU) can also cause your cluster to turn red. A vSphere HA agent can also cause a similar behavior if gets unresponsive. In all these cases, you should follow the guidelines mentioned in the preceding section. You should also ensure that all the hosts that form the clusters are in good health and that the connectivity exists across all the hosts.

The most common error that you are likely to face is when a virtual machine does not start when you attempt to power it on. The virtual machine to be powered on does not satisfy the requirement of resources available and therefore cannot be powered on. The vSphere admission control policy monitors the resources, and in case of insufficient resources, the virtual machine remains switched off. This can happen due to multiple reasons, but most commonly the error comes up when a virtual machine has been allocated a large memory and CPU and the reservations cannot be made due to insufficient resources, for example, a virtual machine with 10 GB of memory on a vSphere host that has 9 GB of memory.

In case **Fault Tolerance** (**FT**)is also turned on, it requires some amount or some percentage of allocated resources to be available on the other host. VMware Fault Tolerance creates a secondary copy of a virtual machine that can replace a primary virtual machine in case of its failure. So when a failure occurs, the virtual machine can be transferred using VMware FT via virtual lockstep or vLockstep (vLockstep records events and inputs for primary virtual machines and sends them to the secondary virtual machines) to another host while keeping the secondary virtual machine in sync with the primary. The secondary virtual machine becomes the primary virtual machine and creates another secondary virtual machine on another host. As I mentioned earlier, if hosts in a cluster are disconnected or are in the maintenance mode, they can also generate the same error. If it is happening because of unavailability of free slots in the cluster, you can reduce the slot size in vSphere HA advanced options. A slot is the amount of reservation of CPU or memory resources for any given virtual machine that a vSphere HA uses. By default, the memory is set to 0 MB + overhead and the CPU is set to 32 MHz if there are no virtual machines in the vSphere cluster. Slot size affects admission control, and you should know how to check the slot size.

Follow these steps to check the slot size in the vSphere web client:

1. Log in to your vSphere web client and click on the vCenter server.

2. Now choose a cluster by expanding your datacenter.

3. Click on the **Monitor** tab and then click on the **vSphere HA** tab.

4. On the right-hand side of the screen, you will see the **Advanced Runtime Info** section.

5. You can find all the information about slot size and how many slots are available in the cluster in this section.

6. Now you can configure the **vSphere HA Advanced Options** to set up an unlimited cap on the slot size.

7. If you see the slot size is in a low count, you can reduce the virtual machine reservations and the use the **vSphere HA Advanced Options** to reduce the slot size.

8. You can also use a different admission control policy to set it up.

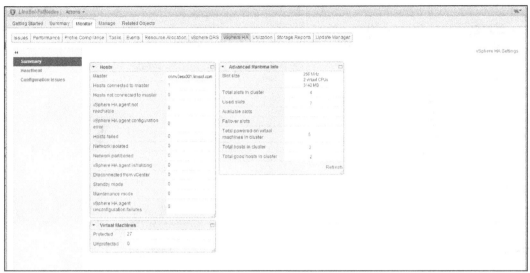

I/O control troubleshooting

In vSphere infrastructure storage, I/O usage of virtual machines can be controlled by **Storage I/O control** (**SIOC**). SIOC delivers storage I/O performance isolation of virtual machines. You can easily run important workloads using SIOC in virtualized storage infrastructure while it stops heavy I/O used virtual machines from impacting on less I/O used virtual machines. You can also allocate a preferred I/O resource for virtual machines using SIOC during bottlenecks. In addition, SIOC can be used to alleviate the poor performance of critical workloads because of I/O bottlenecks and latency in peak times. Some of the features of SIOC are as follows:

- SIOC is disabled by default and needs to be enabled for each datastore in your vSphere infrastructure
- It has a default latency threshold of 30 MS
- It uses disk shares to allocate I/O queue slots
- It does not intervene until the congestion latency threshold is reached and a percentage of the peak performance of a datastore is affected

Follow these steps to enable SIOC:

1. Click on the datastore for which you want to enable SIOC from the vSphere inventory list.

2. Click on the **Configuration** tab.

3. Now, click on **Properties**.

4. Click on the **Enabled** checkbox in the SIOC section to enable it.

5. Click **Close**.

The biggest benefit of enabling the SIOC feature is that it ensures that each VMDK has equal access to the datastore.

If you start having problems after enabling SIOC or the number of vSphere hosts has been changed to SIOC-enabled datastore, disable SIOC and then re-enable it to avoid problems.

SIOC logging

As this book is about troubleshooting, it is very important to enable logging for SIOC for troubleshooting purposes.

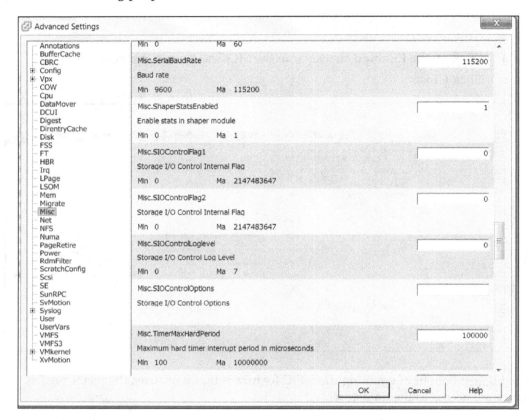

Let's enable SIOC logging from the vSphere client:

1. Open up your vSphere client and log in to it.

2. Click on **Host** and then go to the **Configuration** tab.

3. From the left-hand side column named **Software**, click on **Advanced Settings**. The **Advanced Settings** pop-up will appear.

4. In the parameters list, go down to the **Misc** section and select the **Misc. SIOControlLogLevel** parameter.

5. By default, it is set to zero, which means it is disabled. To log everything, set the value to 7.

6. Enter 7 in the field and click **OK** to close the pop-up box.

7. You will now be able to see the logs in `/var/log/vmkernel`.

Changing vDisk shares and limits for a virtual machine

All virtual machines are allocated the same number of shares and a limited set up for I/O operations per second. When you have several virtual machines accessing the same NFS or VMFS datastores using the same logical unit numbers, you may be required to prioritize the access of the disk shares of your virtual machines. You can change disk share priority from low or normal to high or custom. You can assign the I/O bandwidth of your host disk to the virtual disks of your virtual machines. Be aware that disk I/O is host-specific and cannot be load balanced across a cluster, so shares of a virtual machine on one host do not affect the disk shares of the second. Disk shares can be used to control disk bandwidth of all the virtual machines. Disk share values are measured to the total number of all shares of all the virtual machines on the host.

You can check the shares of virtual machines in a datacenter from Storage as follows:

1. Log in to your vCenter Server and choose the virtual machine you would like to view or change vDisk shares on.

2. Right-click on the selected virtual machine and click **Edit Settings**.

3. Click on the **Resources** tab and select **Disk**.

4. In the **Shares** column, click on the dropdown list and choose the shares amount. You can choose low, normal, or high, or custom to define your own value.

5. To set up an IOPS limit, enter a limit of storage resources in the Limit-IOPS column:

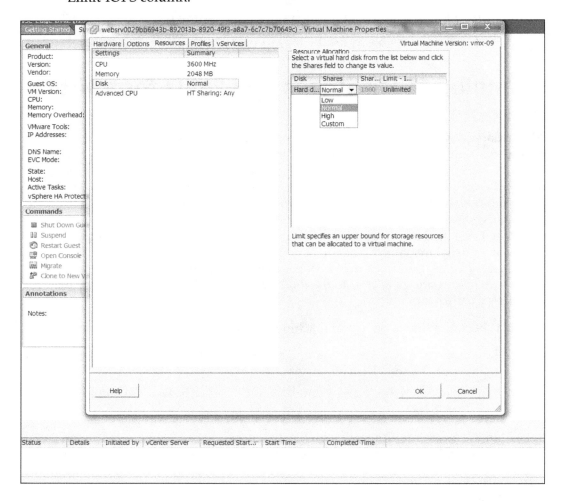

vSphere Fault Tolerance for virtual machines

Fault-tolerant virtual machines are always anticipated in a highly available environment. Fault Tolerance not only ensures high availability but also promises stability for your virtual machines by minimizing the impact of failover rates. The more you use fault tolerance, the more you will need the skills in Fault Tolerance troubleshooting. In the upcoming section, we will discuss some of the most common problems relevant to a virtual machine's fault tolerance and how to troubleshoot them.

Before we get into troubleshooting, here's a list of some best practices for VMware Fault Tolerance configuration to avoid having problems:

- Your cluster should consist of at least three vSphere hosts to provide Fault Tolerance to your infrastructure.

- Always use a dedicated NAS/SAN for your storage environment equipped with at least 1 Gbit NICs.

- Do not use more than 16 virtual disks.

- Your resource pool should have more memory than allocated to fault-tolerant virtual machines in total.

- Do not have more than four fault-tolerant virtual machines on any single host. That includes primary and secondary Fault-Tolerant virtual machines as well. However, the number of virtual machines to run on a single vSphere host depends on workloads of vSphere hosts and virtual machines and can be varied.

- Beware of virtual machines with large memory, as they can prevent you from enabling fault tolerance for your virtual machines.

- Migrating a fault-tolerant virtual machine using vMotion with a large memory can also fail. Further, if the memory is changing at a faster rate than vMotion is copying it over the network, it can result in a failure.

Common troubleshooting of fault tolerance

A common mistake support staff usually makes is enabling vSphere Fault Tolerance without enabling Hardware Virtualization. You enable a virtual machine with Fault Tolerance and you try to power it on, but it generates the following error message: `Hardware Virtualization might not be available either because it is not supported by the vSphere host hardware or because Hardware Virtualization is not enabled in the BIOS.` You should always enable the hardware virtualization within your system's BIOS instead of realizing it at a later stage when your vSphere host is full of virtual machines.

This kind of behavior also occurs when you have your ESXi hosts installed on two different kinds of hardware machines. You attempt to power on a fault-tolerant virtual machine, but it complains about unavailability of compatible hosts where it can run the virtual machine. The same complaint can also appear if hardware virtualization is not enabled on the host, there are no more hosts available, or a host is already in maintenance mode. But if you follow step-by-step troubleshooting techniques, it is not that difficult to find the correct reason.

Another issue that is difficult to understand is when you find that a backup virtual machine is utilizing more CPU than a primary virtual machine, while the primary virtual machine also happens to be idle. You can safely ignore such behavior, as different repetitive events, including interruptions on the backup virtual machine, can keep it busier than the primary virtual machine.

There are also times when you see performance degradation of a primary virtual machine. Though the host hosting the master virtual machine has enough resources, the virtual machine still appears to be operating slowly. In this particular scenario, you should monitor the backup virtual machine to see its resource utilization. You may be surprised to find that the backup virtual machine is utilizing the resources heavily and is overcommitting the CPU resources. This is the reason the master virtual machine slows down and allows the backup virtual machine to run faster.

You can avoid such behavior by allocating enough CPU reservations for the master virtual machine to accommodate the desired workloads. In this case, the reservations are set for both the master and the backup virtual machine so that they can run constantly without any problems.

Enabling fault tolerance can also fail for virtual machines with large memory, as mentioned earlier in the best practices of this section. If that happens to you, turning off your virtual machine and increasing the timeout window for it can solve the problem. The default timeout window is 8 seconds. You can increase this to 30 seconds. Add the following in the vmx file of your virtual machine:

```
ft.maxSwitchoverSeconds = "30"
```

You can use this procedure to enable Fault Tolerance and turn the virtual machine back on, but always consider the tradeoffs before enabling Fault Tolerance.

Configuring SNMP traps for continuous monitoring

VMware ESXi hosts are shipped with SNMP agents that enable ESXi hosts to send SNMP traps and receive information. SNMP is a group of tools and resources to manage networks and can be used for the following functions:

- To monitor CPU, memory, storage, network, and so on
- To keep an eye on your system uptime and connectivity

SNMP is widely adapted and almost all vendors support it, as does VMware.

Configuring SNMP traps with vMA

In the last topic of the chapter, we will configure SNMP traps using the vSphere vMA appliance as follows:

1. Log in to vMA as vi-admin.

2. Add a server as a vMA target by running the following command:

   `vifp addserver crimv3esx002.linxsol.com --authpolicy fpauth`

3. Now, set it as the target server to perform operations:

   `vifptarget --set crimv3esx002.linxsol.com`

4. Once the target is set, simply type the following command in the console to set up the SNMP community string:

   `vicfg-snmp -c public01`

5. Configure the SNMP agent to send SNMP traps on UDP Port 162. The SNMP agents receive requests on UDP Port 161 while SNMP agents send their response to SNMP manager on Port 162. Type the following in the console:

   `vicfg-snmp -t 192.168.0.142@162/public01`

6. Enable the ESXi SNMP agent by running the following command:

   `vicfg-snmp --enable`

7. Verify that the SNMP traps are running fine using the following command:

   `vicfg-snmp -test`

```
login as: vi-admin
Welcome to vSphere Management Assistant
Using keyboard-interactive authentication.
Password:
Last login: Mon Apr 13 19:18:38 2015 from 10.5.2.77
vi-admin@vma:~> vicfg-snmp --help

Synopsis: /usr/bin/vicfg-snmp OPTIONS


Command-specific options:
   --communities
    -c
       Set communities separated by comma comm1[,...] (this overwrites previous
settings)
   --disable
    -D
      Stop SNMP service
   --enable
```

8. For additional information, you can run the `vicfg-snmp` command with the help switch:

```
vicfg-snmp --help
```

 Use the ping command to ping the SNMP receiver from the vCenter Server to verify that the connectivity exists before proceeding.

Tuning the SNMP agents

You can follow these instructions to set up an SNMP agent using VMware vAdmin:

1. Log in to vMA as vi-admin.

2. Add a server as a vMA target by running the following command:

```
vifp addserver crimv3esx002.linxsol.com --authpolicy fpauth
```

3. Now, set it as the target server to perform operations:

```
vifptarget --set crimv3esx002.linxsol.com
```

4. Once the target is set, simply type the following command in the console to set up the SNMP agent to answer other requests generated by other devices— by default, the SNMP agent listens on Port 1611 UDP. Type the following to change it to 1611:

```
vicfg-snmp -p 1611
```

5. Now, configure the SNMP agent to use CIM to receive events from the hardware sensors:

```
vicfg-snmp -y indications
```

6. Let's view the SNMP configuration information so far:

```
vicfg-snmp --show
```

```
vifp          vifptarget  vifs
vi-admin@vma:~> vifp listservers
crimv1vcs001.linxsol.com    vCenter
crimv3esx001.linxsol.com    ESXi
crimv3esx002.linxsol.com    ESXi
vi-admin@vma:~> vifptarget --set crimv3esx002.linxsol.com
vi-admin@vma:~[crimv3esx002.linxsol.com]> vicfg-snmp -c community1
Changing community list to: community1...
Complete.
vi-admin@vma:~[crimv3esx002.linxsol.com]> vicfg-snmp -t 10.2.6.91@
162/community1
Changing notification(trap) targets list to: 10.2.6.91@162/community1...
Complete.
vi-admin@vma:~[crimv3esx002.linxsol.com]> vicfg-snmp --enable
Enabling agent...
Complete.
vi-admin@vma:~[crimv3esx002.linxsol.com]>
```

Configuring SNMP agents from PowerCLI

Let's walk through configuring an SNMP agent for ESXi hosts using PowerCLI:

1. Open your PowerCLI console.

2. Connect with the ESXi host you would like to enable the SNMP agent on and when prompted, enter the valid credentials for your ESXi host.

3. Connect to VIServer `crimv3esx002.linxsol.com`

4. Whether the SNMP agent has been configured already or not, you can view its configuration by typing the following in the PowerCLI console:

   Get-VMHostSnmp

5. If the SNMP agent has not already been enabled, you can enable it as follows:

   Get-VMHostSnmp | Set-VMHostSnmp -enabled:$true

6. Once it is configured, you can test it as follows:

```
Get-VMHostSnmp | Test-VMHostSnmp
```

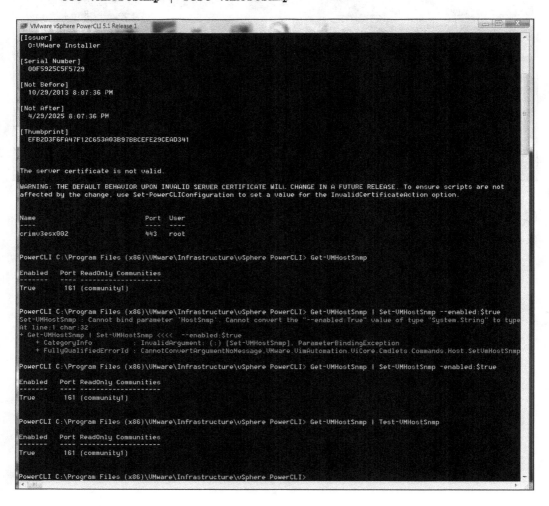

 You can manually change SNMP configuration in a vSphere host by editing the /etc/vmware/snmp.xml file. The SNMP agent of a vSphere host logs all messages to /var/log/syslog.log.

Summary

In this chapter, you learned how to obtain basic information about clusters in order to troubleshoot their common problems. You also learned how this information can be used in advance to prevent any problems from occurring later. Performance monitoring of cluster is a very important ingredient, and it helps you with your business continuity and with managing workloads.

The topic of troubleshooting the heartbeat datastore and DRS storage issues provided a basic insight about some of the very common problems occurring in these areas, how to solve them, and some tips to prevent them from happening. I also covered troubleshooting tips on managing resources, especially when there aren't enough available. Configuring SNMP traps help resource monitoring at one place and you can configure them further to receive severe alerts by texts or email.

4
Monitoring and Troubleshooting Networking

Monitoring and troubleshooting vSphere networking, which includes troubleshooting vSphere virtual distributed switches, vSphere standard virtual switches, vLANs, uplinks, DNS, and routing, is one of the core issues a seasoned system engineer has to deal with on a daily basis. This chapter will cover all these topics and give you hands-on step-by-step instructions to manage and monitor your network resources. By the end of this chapter, you will be able to troubleshoot networking issues and apply networking best practices to your vSphere infrastructure. You will learn about the log files relevant to vSphere networking and basic vSphere network switching concepts in the first section. In the second section, you will learn network-troubleshooting commands and apply the troubleshooting commands from vCLI, PowerCLI, and the VMware vMA appliance to troubleshoot vSphere networking. The following topics will be covered in this chapter:

- Networking log files
- Different network troubleshooting commands
- VLANs troubleshooting
- Verification of physical trunks and VLAN configuration
- Testing of VM connectivity
- VMkernel interface troubleshooting
- Configuration command (`Vicfg-vmknic` and `esxcli network ip` interface)
- Use of **Direct Console User Interface (DCUI)** to verify configuration
- Port mirroring troubleshooting
- NetFlow configuration
- DNS and routing troubleshooting
- DNS troubleshooting commands

Log files

You can find information about all DHCP-related issues in the `/var/log/dhclient.log` file. The file includes information about how a VMkernel interface acquires an IP address and how it performs the renewal. In the following screenshot, you can see `DHCPREQUEST, DHCPDISCOVER` on `vmk0` messages to be broadcasted.

Initially, a `DHCPDISCOVER` broadcast message is sent by the VMkernel client interface. The `DHCPDISCOVER` message then tries to look around for a DHCP server, and if found, the VMkernel client interface requests for an IP address. You can see in the screenshot, the broadcast request is being sent on `255.255.255.255`. If no DHCP server is available to offer a lease, you will see a `No DHCPOFFERS received` message once it times out. If a DHCP offer has been made by a DHCP server, the server will send a unicast message of `DHCPOFFERS` to the client.

The vSphere client tries to renew its DHCP state and unicasts a `DHCPREQUEST` to the DHCP server at a time interval of `interval1` multiplied by the duration of the lease. The lease is then extended by the DHCP server. All these requests are logged in `/var/log/dhclient.log`.

You can check the log file if you face problems in getting an IP address assigned, or if any IP address conflicts occur on the network. You can also check if the DHCP lease is not renewed. All such requests are logged into `/var/log/dhclient.log`. The VMkernel cannot renew or extend its lease if your DHCP server is located in another subnet, as it cannot reach the DHCP server by unicast. You must always make sure that your DHCP has been assigned an interface on the subnet where the VMkernel port is allowed to perform DHCP renewals by unicast messages. The `/var/log/dhclient.log` file records a lot of interesting information, for example, when a vSphere host reboots or you restart the management network; when a reversed DNS look is performed; or when a PTR record is being resolved.

Another important file you should be aware of is `/var/log/vmkwarning.log`. Whenever there are critical warnings from the `vmkernel` log, they appear in `vmkwarning`. This file is much easier to read as compared to `/var/log/vmkernel.log`.

```
2013-10-30T07:46:52Z dhclient-uw[8861]: DHCPDISCOVER on vmk0 to 255.255.255.255 port 67 interval 5
2013-10-30T07:46:57Z dhclient-uw[8861]: DHCPDISCOVER on vmk0 to 255.255.255.255 port 67 interval 7
2013-10-30T07:47:04Z dhclient-uw[8861]: DHCPDISCOVER on vmk0 to 255.255.255.255 port 67 interval 18
2013-10-30T07:47:22Z dhclient-uw[8861]: DHCPDISCOVER on vmk0 to 255.255.255.255 port 67 interval 20
2013-10-30T07:47:42Z dhclient-uw[8861]: DHCPDISCOVER on vmk0 to 255.255.255.255 port 67 interval 10
2013-10-30T07:47:52Z dhclient-uw[8861]: DHCPDISCOVER on vmk0 to 255.255.255.255 port 67 interval 7
2013-10-30T07:47:59Z dhclient-uw[8861]: DHCPDISCOVER on vmk0 to 255.255.255.255 port 67 interval 7
2013-10-30T07:48:06Z dhclient-uw[8861]: DHCPDISCOVER on vmk0 to 255.255.255.255 port 67 interval 14
2013-10-30T07:48:20Z dhclient-uw[8861]: DHCPDISCOVER on vmk0 to 255.255.255.255 port 67 interval 3
2013-10-30T07:48:23Z dhclient-uw[8861]: No DHCPOFFERS received.
2013-10-30T07:48:23Z dhclient-uw[8861]: No working leases in persistent database - sleeping.
2013-10-30T07:48:23Z dhclient-uw[8861]: system command failed. The command is: /usr/lib/vmware/vob/bin/addvob vob.user
one 'vmk0'
2013-10-30T07:49:38Z dhclient-uw[8861]: DHCPDISCOVER on vmk0 to 255.255.255.255 port 67 interval 6
2013-10-30T07:49:44Z dhclient-uw[8861]: DHCPDISCOVER on vmk0 to 255.255.255.255 port 67 interval 10
2013-10-30T07:49:54Z dhclient-uw[8861]: DHCPDISCOVER on vmk0 to 255.255.255.255 port 67 interval 20
2013-10-30T07:50:14Z dhclient-uw[8861]: DHCPDISCOVER on vmk0 to 255.255.255.255 port 67 interval 18
2013-10-30T07:50:32Z dhclient-uw[8861]: DHCPDISCOVER on vmk0 to 255.255.255.255 port 67 interval 10
2013-10-30T07:50:42Z dhclient-uw[8861]: DHCPDISCOVER on vmk0 to 255.255.255.255 port 67 interval 7
2013-10-30T07:50:49Z dhclient-uw[8861]: DHCPDISCOVER on vmk0 to 255.255.255.255 port 67 interval 11
2013-10-30T07:51:00Z dhclient-uw[8861]: DHCPDISCOVER on vmk0 to 255.255.255.255 port 67 interval 9
2013-10-30T07:51:09Z dhclient-uw[8861]: No DHCPOFFERS received.
2013-10-30T07:51:09Z dhclient-uw[8861]: No working leases in persistent database - sleeping.
2013-10-30T07:51:09Z dhclient-uw[8861]: system command failed. The command is: /usr/lib/vmware/vob/bin/addvob vob.user
one 'vmk0'
2013-10-30T07:52:27Z dhclient-uw[8861]: DHCPDISCOVER on vmk0 to 255.255.255.255 port 67 interval 8
2013-10-30T07:52:35Z dhclient-uw[8861]: DHCPDISCOVER on vmk0 to 255.255.255.255 port 67 interval 14
2013-10-30T07:52:49Z dhclient-uw[8861]: DHCPDISCOVER on vmk0 to 255.255.255.255 port 67 interval 14
2013-10-30T07:53:03Z dhclient-uw[8861]: DHCPDISCOVER on vmk0 to 255.255.255.255 port 67 interval 17
2013-10-30T07:53:20Z dhclient-uw[8861]: DHCPDISCOVER on vmk0 to 255.255.255.255 port 67 interval 21
2013-10-30T07:53:41Z dhclient-uw[8861]: DHCPDISCOVER on vmk0 to 255.255.255.255 port 67 interval 17
2013-10-30T07:53:58Z dhclient-uw[8861]: No DHCPOFFERS received.
2013-10-30T07:53:58Z dhclient-uw[8861]: No working leases in persistent database - sleeping.
2013-10-30T07:53:58Z dhclient-uw[8861]: system command failed. The command is: /usr/lib/vmware/vob/bin/addvob vob.user
one 'vmk0'
2013-10-30T07:54:34Z dhclient-uw[8861]: DHCPDISCOVER on vmk0 to 255.255.255.255 port 67 interval 7
```

Another log file is `/var/log/vpxa.log`, which records the logs about the vpxa agent. This file also logs hosted host management and communication of vCenter Server with vSphere.

Network driver and device type issues `/var/log/vmkernel.log`, perform the following steps:

1. Open your PowerCLI console.
2. Connect with the ESXi host on which you would like to enable the SNMP agent, and when prompted, enter the valid credentials for your ESXi host.
3. Connect to VIServer `crimv3esx002.linxsol.com`.

VMware vSphere uses two types of virtualized switches: standard switches and distributed switches. These switches have port groups and ports in order to allow connectivity. You must have some basic understanding of how switches work in order to troubleshoot.

Network traffic is routed locally to the virtual machines connected by a virtual switch, which are on the same VLAN or a port group. For external network access, virtual machines connected by a virtual switch use an uplink, and the adapter is connected to either a standard virtual switch or a distributed virtual switch.

The vSphere standard switch allows your virtual machines to connect to an external network, as you can see in the following screenshot:

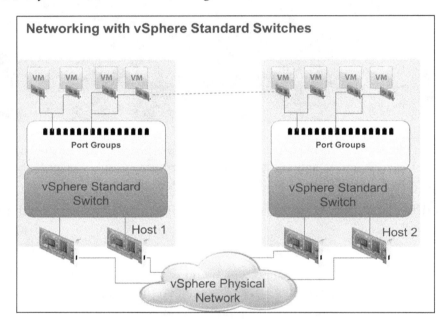

Virtual machines use distributed switches in order to maintain their network settings and therefore migrate without any problem. The upcoming screenshot depicts how a distributed switch works. The physical network cards are connected with vSphere hosts as uplinks, and a distributed switch is connected with virtual machines' NICs to provide connectivity. The virtual machine networking is now distributed and independent of the vSphere host.

The benefit of this approach is that you don't need to worry about your virtual machine's network configuration. The network configuration remains consistent when you migrate a virtual machine from one vSphere host to another vSphere host.

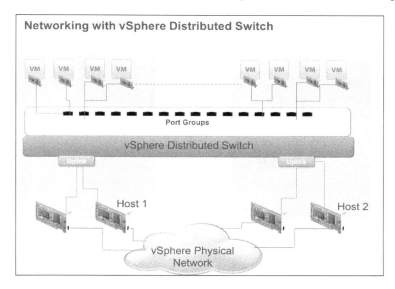

Understanding the virtual network creation process

Before we move on to discuss in detail network troubleshooting commands, we should have a basic understanding of how virtual networks are created in vSphere. This can be done by the following:

- Create a virtual switch
- Configure your uplink adapters
- Add port groups to the virtual switch
- Associate VLAN with the virtual switch, if any
- Configure VMkernel interfaces

Network troubleshooting commands

Some of the commands that can be used for networking troubleshooting include net-dvs, Esxcli network, vicfg-route, vicfg-vmknic, vicfg-dns, vicfg-nics, and vicfg-vswitch.

You can use the net-dvs command to troubleshoot VMware distributed dvSwitches. The command shows all the information regarding the VMware distributed dvSwtich configuration. The net-dvs command reads the information from the /etc/vmware/dvsdata.db file and displays all the data in the console. A vSphere host keeps updating its dvsdata.db file every five minutes.

1. Connect to a vSphere host using PuTTY.

2. Enter your user name and password when prompted.

3. Type the following command in the CLI:

   net-dvs

4. You will see something similar to the following screenshot:

```
~ # net-dvs
switch 67 bc 2f 50 84 a1 77 ef-a5 73 b3 ca 9f e3 4b 64 (etherswitch)
        max ports: 512
        global properties:
                com.vmware.common.version = 0x 2. 0. 0. 0
                        propType = CONFIG
                com.vmware.common.alias = dvSwitch-External-Networks ,   propType = CONFIG
                com.vmware.etherswitch.mtu = 1500 ,        propType = CONFIG
                com.vmware.etherswitch.cdp = CDP, listen
                        propType = CONFIG
                com.vmware.common.respools.list:
                        netsched.pools.persist.ft
                        netsched.pools.persist.hbr
                        netsched.pools.persist.iscsi
                        netsched.pools.persist.mgmt
                        netsched.pools.persist.nfs
                        netsched.pools.persist.vm
                        netsched.pools.persist.vmotion
                        netsched.pools.persist.vsan
                        propType = CONFIG
                com.vmware.common.respools.sched:
                        active
                        propType = CONFIG
                com.vmware.etherswitch.ipv4addr = 0.0.0.0,        propType = CONFIG
                com.vmware.common.uplinkPorts:
                        dvUplink1, dvUplink2
                        propType = CONFIG
                com.vmware.etherswitch.ipfix:
                        idle timeout = 15 seconds
                        active timeout = 60 seconds
                        sampling rate = 0
                        collector = 0.0.0.0:2311
                        internal flows only = false
                        propType = CONFIG
        host properties:
                com.vmware.common.host.portset = DvsPortset-0 ,          propType = CONFIG
```

In the preceding screenshot, you can see that the first line represents the UUID of a VMware distributed switch. The second line shows the maximum number of ports a distributed switch can have. The line `com.vmware.common.alias = dvswitch-Network-Pools` represents the name of a distributed switch. The next line `com.vmware.common.uplinkPorts: dvUplink1` to `dvUplinkn` shows the uplink ports a distributed switch has. The distributed switch MTU is set to 1,600 and you can see the information about CDP just below it. CDP information can be useful to troubleshoot connectivity issues.

You can see `com.vmware.common.respools.list` listing networking resource pools, while `com.vmware.common.host.uplinkPorts` shows the ports numbers assigned to uplink ports. Further details about these uplink ports are explained as follows for each uplink port by their port number. You can also see the port statistics as displayed in the following screenshot. When you perform troubleshooting, these statistics can help you to check the behavior of the distributed switch and the ports. From these statistics, you can diagnose if the data packets are going in and out. As you can see in the following screenshot, all the metrics regarding packet drops are zero. If you find in your troubleshooting that the packets are being dropped, you can easily start finding the root cause of the problem:

```
10.2.6.30 - PuTTY
        com.vmware.common.port.statistics:
            pktsInUnicast = 8732418723
            bytesInUnicast = 9268326389939
            pktsInMulticast = 6569431
            bytesInMulticast = 1721248420
            pktsInBroadcast = 46188401
            bytesInBroadcast = 2800175462
            pktsOutUnicast = 2790264214
            bytesOutUnicast = 5146471918663
            pktsOutMulticast = 151
            bytesOutMulticast = 14365
            pktsOutBroadcast = 114254
            bytesOutBroadcast = 6855240
            pktsInDropped = 0
            pktsOutDropped = 0
            pktsInException = 6
            pktsOutException = 0
            propType = RUNTIME
        com.vmware.common.port.volatile.vlan = VLAN 0
            ranges = 0-4094
```

Unfortunately, the `net-dvs` command is very poorly documented, and usually, it is hard to find useful references. Moreover, it is not supported by VMware. However, you can use it with `-h` switch to display more options.

```
10.2.6.30 - PuTTY
/var/log # net-dvs -h
Warning: This is an unsupported command. Use at your own risk.
net-dvs -a [ -P maxPorts] switch_name          add a new dvswitch
net-dvs -d switch_name                          delete a dvswitch
net-dvs [ -A | -D ] -p port switch_name        add/delete a port from a dvswitch
net-dvs [ -s name=value | -u name ] -p port switch_name
                                                set/unset key/value pair property for dvport
net-dvs -r name -p port switch_name            get value for dvport property specified
net-dvs -l [ switch_name ]                      list dvs information
net-dvs -i                                      init database
net-dvs [-S | -R | -G ]                         set vmkernel state from config file/reset
                                                vmkernel state/get dvs state from vmkernel
                                                to config file
net-dvs -T                                      test dvsdata
net-dvs -v "vlanID[;t|p[0-7][;min-max,min-max...]]
                                                set vlan configuration
net-dvs -V "primaryVID,secondaryVID,i|c|p;primaryVID,secondaryVID,i|c|p..."
                                                set PVLAN global table contents
net-dvs -E /path/acl_file -I "com.vmware.etherswitch.port.acl.output"
       -p dvport switch_name
                                                set acl to filter dvport's egress traffic
net-dvs -E /path/acl_file -I "com.vmware.etherswitch.port.acl.input"
       -p dvport switch_name
                                                set acl to filter dvport's ingress traffic
       acl_file should be written with the following keywords:
       numACLs:         (required)the total number of acls in this file
```

Repairing a dvsdata.db file

Sometimes, the `dvsdata.db` file of a vSphere host becomes corrupted and you face different types of distributed switch errors, for example, unable to create proxy DVS. In this case, when you try to run the `net-dvs` command on a vSphere host, it will fail with an error as well. As I have mentioned earlier, the `net-dvs` command reads data from the `/etc/vmware/dvsdata.db` file — it fails because it is unable to read data from the file. The possible cause for the corruption of the `dvsdata.db` file could be network outage; or when a vSphere host is disconnected from vCenter and deleted, it might have the information in its cache.

You can resolve this issue by restoring the `dvsdata.db` file by following these steps:

1. Through PuTTY, connect to a functioning vSphere host in your infrastructure.

2. Copy the `dvsdata.db` file from the vSphere host. The file can be found in `/etc/vmware/dvsdata.db`.

3. Transfer the copied `dvsdata.db` file to the corrupted vSphere host and overwrite it.

4. Restart your vSphere host.

5. Once the vSphere host is up and running, use PuTTY to connect to it.

6. Run the `net-dvs` command. The command should be executed successfully this time without any errors.

ESXCLI network

The `esxcli network` command is a longtime friend of the system administrator and the support staff for troubleshooting network related issues. The `esxcli network` command will be used to examine different network configurations and to troubleshoot problems. You can type `esxcli network` to quickly see a help reference and the different options that can be used with the command.

Let's walk through some useful esxcli network troubleshooting commands. Type the following command into your vSphere CLI to list all the virtual machines and the networks they are on. You can see that the command returned `World ID`, virtual machine name, number of ports, and the network:

```
esxcli network vm list

World ID   Name   Num Ports   Networks

--------   ------------------------------------------------------   ---------
----------------

14323012   cluster08_(5fa21117-18f7-427c-84d1-c63922199e05)              1
dvportgroup-372
```

Now use the `World ID` of a virtual machine returned by the last command to list all the ports the virtual machine is currently using. You can see the virtual switch name, MAC address of the NIC, IP address, and uplink port ID:

```
esxcli network vm port list -w 14323012
   Port ID: 50331662
   vSwitch: dvSwitch-Network-Pools
   Portgroup: dvportgroup-372
   DVPort ID: 1063
   MAC Address: 00:50:56:01:00:7e
   IP Address: 0.0.0.0
   Team Uplink: all(2)
   Uplink Port ID: 0
   Active Filters:
```

Type the following command in the CLI to list the statistics of the virtual switch—you need to replace the port ID as returned by the last command after -p flag:

```
esxcli network port stats get -p 50331662
Packet statistics for port 50331662
    Packets received: 10787391024
    Packets sent: 7661812086
    Bytes received: 3048720170788
    Bytes sent: 154147668506
    Broadcast packets received: 17831672
    Broadcast packets sent: 309404
    Multicast packets received: 656
    Multicast packets sent: 52
    Unicast packets received: 10769558696
    Unicast packets sent: 7661502630
    Receive packets dropped: 92865923
    Transmit packets dropped: 0
```

Type the following command to list complete information about the network card of the virtual machine:

```
esxcli network nic stats get -n vmnic0
NIC statistics for vmnic0
    Packets received: 2969343419
    Packets sent: 155331621
    Bytes received: 2264469102098
    Bytes sent: 46007679331
    Receive packets dropped: 0
    Transmit packets dropped: 0
    Total receive errors: 78507
    Receive length errors: 0
    Receive over errors: 22
    Receive CRC errors: 0
    Receive frame errors: 0
    Receive FIFO errors: 78485
    Receive missed errors: 0
    Total transmit errors: 0
    Transmit aborted errors: 0
```

```
Transmit carrier errors: 0

Transmit FIFO errors: 0

Transmit heartbeat errors: 0

Transmit window errors: 0
```

```
~ # esxcli network vm list
World ID  Name                                                        Num Ports  Networks
--------  ----------------------------------------------------------  ---------  ---------------
14323012       cluster08_(5fa21117-18f7-427c-84d1-c63922199e05)              1  dvportgroup-372
~ # esxcli network vm port list -w 14323012
   Port ID: 50331662
   vSwitch: dvSwitch-Network-Pools
   Portgroup: dvportgroup-372
   DVPort ID: 1063
   MAC Address: 00:50:56:01:00:7e
   IP Address: 0.0.0.0
   Team Uplink: all(2)
   Uplink Port ID: 0
   Active Filters:
~ # esxcli network port stats get -p 50331662
Packet statistics for port 50331662
   Packets received: 10787391024
   Packets sent: 7661812086
   Bytes received: 3048720170788
   Bytes sent: 154147668506
   Broadcast packets received: 17831672
   Broadcast packets sent: 309404
   Multicast packets received: 656
   Multicast packets sent: 52
   Unicast packets received: 10769558696
   Unicast packets sent: 7661502630
   Receive packets dropped: 92865923
   Transmit packets dropped: 0
~ # esxcli network port filter stats get -p 50331662
~ # esxcli network nic stats get -n vmnic0
NIC statistics for vmnic0
   Packets received: 2969343419
   Packets sent: 155331621
   Bytes received: 2264469102098
   Bytes sent: 46007679331
   Receive packets dropped: 0
   Transmit packets dropped: 0
   Total receive errors: 78507
   Receive length errors: 0
   Receive over errors: 22
   Receive CRC errors: 0
   Receive frame errors: 0
   Receive FIFO errors: 78485
   Receive missed errors: 0
   Total transmit errors: 0
   Transmit aborted errors: 0
   Transmit carrier errors: 0
   Transmit FIFO errors: 0
   Transmit heartbeat errors: 0
   Transmit window errors: 0
~ # 
```

 A complete reference of the ESXCli network command can be found here at `https://goo.gl/9OMbVU`.

All the `vicfg-*` commands are very helpful and easy to use. It is out of the scope of this book to cover all the commands. But I will encourage you to learn in order to make your life easier. Here are some of the `vicfg-*` commands relevant to network troubleshooting:

- `vicfg-route`: We will discuss this command later in the chapter, how to add or remove IP routes, and how to create and delete default IP gateways.

- `vicfg-vmknic`: We will use this command to perform different operations on VMkernel NICs for vSphere hosts.

- `vicfg-dns`: This command will be used to manipulate DNS information. We will discuss it later in the chapter.

- `vicfg-nics`: We will use this command to manipulate vSphere physical NICs.

- `vicfg-vswitch`: We will use this command to to create, delete, and modify `vswitch` information.

Troubleshooting uplinks

We will use the `vicfg-nics` command to manage physical network adapters of vSphere hosts. The `vicfg-nics` command can also be used to set up the speed, VMkernel name for the uplink adapters, duplex setting, driver information, and link state information of the NIC.

Connect to your vMA appliance console and set up the target vSphere host:

```
vifptarget --set crimv3esx001.linxsol.com
```

List all the network cards available in the vSphere host. See the following screenshot for the output:

```
vicfg-nics -l
```

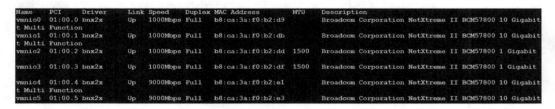

You can see that my vSphere host has five network cards from `vmnic0` to `vmnic5`. You are able to see the PCI and driver information. The link state for the all the network cards is up. You can also see two types of network card speeds: `1000 Mbs` and `9000 Mbs`. There is also a card name in the `Description` field, MTU, and the Mac address for the network cards. You can set up a network card to auto-negotiate as follows:

```
vicfg-nics --auto vimnic0
```

Now let's set the speed of `vmnic0` to `1000` and its duplex settings to full:

```
vicfg-nics --duplex full --speed 1000 vmnic0
```

Troubleshooting virtual switches

The last command we will discuss in this chapter is `vicfg-vswitch`. The `vicfg-vswitch` command is a very powerful command that can be used to manipulate the day-to-day operations of a virtual switch. I will show you how to create and configure port groups and virtual switches.

Set up a vSphere host in the vMA appliance in which you want to get information about virtual switches:

```
vifptarget --set crimv3esx001.linxsol.com
```

Type the following command to list all the information about the switches the vSphere host has. You can see the command output in the screenshot that follows:

```
vicfg-vswitch -l
```

```
vi-admin@vma:~[ crimv3esx001.linxsol.com > vicfg-vswitch -l
Enter username: root
Enter password:
Switch Name      Num Ports      Used Ports      Configured Ports    MTU      Uplinks
vSwitch0         128            7               128                 1500     vmnic2,vmnic3

    PortGroup Name                VLAN ID   Used Ports    Uplinks
    vMotion                       2231      1             vmnic2,vmnic3
    Management Network            2230      1             vmnic3,vmnic2

DVS Name              Num Ports   Used Ports   Configured Ports   Uplinks
OpenStack             512         4            512

    DVPort ID          In Use       Client
    130                0
    132                0
    0                  1           keystone.linxsol.com.eth1
dvSwitch-External-Networks512      5            512                vmnic0,vmnic1

    DVPort ID          In Use       Client
    48                 1           vmnic0
    49                 1           vmnic1
dvSwitch-Network-Pools   512       13           512                vmnic4,vmnic5

    DVPort ID          In Use       Client
    0                  1           vmnic4
    1                  1           vmnic5
    10                 1           vmk2
    921                0
    922                0
    923                0
    920                0
    1137               1           nova (a802a868-9bc8-4777-8fa5-279adef82cc4).eth1
    1131               1           keystone (66f3d6d5-b43e-4426-b5ab-e9960d49b9b0).eth0
    1175               0
    1158               1
vi-admin@vma:~[ crimv3esx001.linxsol.com >
```

You can see that the vSphere host has one virtual switch and two virtual NICs carrying traffic for the management network and for the vMotion. The virtual switch has 128 ports, and seven of them are in a used state. There are two uplinks to the switch with MTU set to 1500, while two VLANS are being used: one for the management network and one for the vMotion traffic. You can also see three distributed switches named OpenStack, dvSwitch-External-Networks, and dvSwitch-Network-Pools.

 Prefixing dv with the distributed switch name is a command practice, and it can help you to easily recognize a distributed switch.

I will go through adding a new virtual switch:

```
vicfg-vswitch --add vSwitch002
```

This creates a virtual switch with 128 ports and an MTU of 1500. You can use the `--mtu` flag to specify a different MTU. Now add an uplink adapter `vnic02` to the newly created virtual switch `vSwitch002`:

```
vicfg-vswitch --link vmnic0 vSwitch002
```

To add a port group to the virtual switch, use the following command:

```
vicfg-vswitch --add-pg portgroup002 vSwitch002
```

Now add an uplink adapter to the port group:

```
vicfg-vswitch --add-pg-uplink vmnic0 --pg portgroup002 vSwitch002
```

We have discussed all the commands to create a virtual switch and its port groups and to add uplinks. Now we will see how to delete and edit the configuration of a virtual switch. An uplink NIC from the port group can be deleted using –N flag. Remove `vmnic0` from the `portgroup002`:

```
vicfg-vswitch --del-pg-uplink vmnic0 --pg portgroup002 vSwitch002
```

You can delete the recently created port group as follows:

```
vicfg-vswitch --del-pg portgroup002 vSwitch002
```

To delete a switch, you first need to remove an uplink adapter from the virtual switch. You need to use the –U flag, which unlinks the uplink from the switch:

```
vicfg-vswitch --unlink vmnic0 vSwitch002
```

You can delete a virtual switch using the –d flag. Here is how you do it:

```
vicfg-vswitch --delete vSwitch002
```

You can check the **Cisco Discovery Protocol (CDP)** settings by using the `--get-cdp` flag with the `vicfg-vswitch` command. The following command resulted in putting the CDP in the `Listen` state, which indicates that the vSphere host is configured to receive CDP information from the physical switch:

```
vi-admin@vma:~[crimv3esx001.linxsol.com] > vicfg-vswitch --get-cdp
vSwitch0

listen
```

You can configure CDP options for the vSphere host to down, listen, or advertise. In the `Listen` mode, the vSphere host tries to discover and publish this information received from a Cisco switch port, though the information of the vSwitch cannot be seen by the Cisco device. In the `Advertise` mode, the vSphere host doesn't discover and publish the information about the Cisco switch; instead, it publishes information about its vSwitch to the Cisco switch device.

```
vicfg-vswitch --set-cdp both vSwitch0
```

Troubleshooting VLANs

Virtual LANS or VLANs are used to separate the physical switching segment into different logical switching segments in order to segregate the broadcast domains. VLANs not only provide network segmentation but also provide us a method of effective network management. It also increases the overall network security, and nowadays, it is very commonly used in infrastructure. If not set up correctly, it can lead your vSphere host to have no connectivity, and you can face some very common problems where you are unable to ping or resolve the hostnames anymore. Some common errors are exposed, such as `Destination host unreachable` and `Connection failed`. A **Private VLAN** (**PVLAN**) is an extended version of VLAN that divides logical broadcast domain into further segments and forms private groups. PVLANs are divided into primary and secondary PVLANs.

Primary PVLAN is the VLAN distributed into smaller segments that are called primary. These then host all the secondary PVLANs within them. Secondary PVLANs live within primary VLANS, and individual secondary VLANs are recognized by VLAN IDs linked to them. Just like their ancestor VLANs, the packets that travel within secondary VLANS are tagged with their associated IDs. Then, the physical switch recognizes if the packets are tagged as isolated, community, or promiscuous.

As network troubleshooting involves taking care of many different aspects, one aspect you will come across in the troubleshooting cycle is actually troubleshooting VLANS. vSphere Enterprise Plus licensing is a requirement to connect a host using a virtual distributed switch and VLANs. You can see the three different network segments in the following screenshot. **VLAN A** connects all the virtual machines on different vSphere hosts; **VLAN B** is responsible for carrying out management network traffic; and **VLAN C** is responsible for carrying out vMotion-related traffic. In order to create PVLANs on your vSphere host, you also need the support of a physical switch:

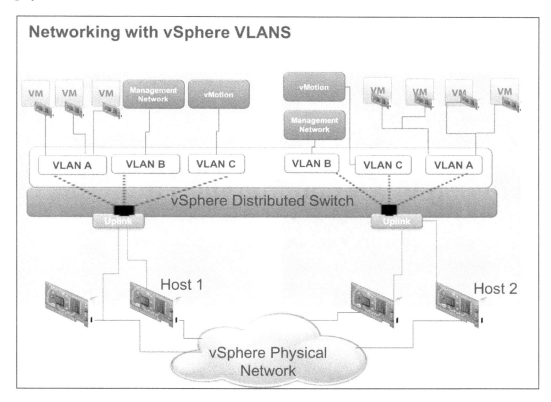

 For detailed information about the vSphere network, refer to the VMware official networking guide for vSphere 5.5 at http:// goo.gl/SYySFL.

Verifying physical trunks and VLAN configuration

The first and most important step to troubleshooting your VLAN problem is to look into the VLAN configuration of your vSphere host. You should always start by verifying it. Let's walk through how to verify the network configuration of the management network and VLAN configuration from the vSphere client:

1. Open and log in to your vSphere client.

2. Click on the vSphere host you are trying to troubleshoot.

3. Click on the **Configuration** menu and choose **Networking** and then **Properties** of the switch you are troubleshooting.

4. Choose the network you are troubleshooting from the list, and click on **Edit**.

5. This will open a new window. Verify the **VLAN ID for Management Network**.

6. Match the ID of the VLAN provided by your network administrator.

Verifying VLAN configuration from CLI

Following are the steps for verifying VLAN configuration from CLI:

1. Log in to vSphere CLI. Type the following command in the console:

   `esxcfg-vswitch -1`

2. Alternatively, in the vMA appliance, type the `vicfg-vswitch` command — the output is similar for both commands:

   `vicfg-vswitch -1`

3. The output of the `excfg-vswitch -1` command is as follows:

Switch Name Uplinks	Num Ports	Used Ports	Configured Ports	MTU
vSwitch0 vmnic3,vmnic2	128	7	128	1500

PortGroup Name	VLAN ID	Used Ports	Uplinks
vMotion	2231	1	vmnic3,vmnic2
Management Network	2230	1	vmnic3,vmnic2

   `---Omitted output---`

4. The output of the `vicfg-vswitch -l` command is as follows:

```
Switch Name       Num Ports        Used Ports         Configured Ports
MTU      Uplinks

vSwitch0          128              7                  128
1500     vmnic2,vmnic3


    PortGroup Name                    VLAN ID    Used Ports      Uplinks
    vMotion                           2231       1
vmnic2,vmnic3

    Management Network                2230       1
vmnic3,vmnic2

--Omitted output---
```

5. Match it with your network configuration. If the VLAN ID is incorrect or missing, you can add or edit it using the following command from the vSphere CLI:

```
esxcfg-vswitch -v 2233 -p "Management Network" vSwitch0
```

6. To add or edit the VLAN ID from the vMA appliance, use the following command:

```
vicfg-vswitch --vlan 2233 --pg "Management Network" vSwitch0
```

Verifying VLANs from PowerCLI

Verifying information about VLANs from the PowerCLI is fairly simple. Type the following command into the console after connecting with vCenter using Connect-VIServer:

```
Get-VirtualPortGroup -VMHost crimv3esx001.linxsol.com | select Name,
VirtualSwitch VLanID


Name                                        VirtualSwitch
VlanId

----                                                    ------------
-                                     -----
vMotion                                              vSwitch0
2231

Management Network                     vSwitch0
2233
```

Verifying PVLANs and secondary PVLANs

When you have configured PVLANs or secondary PVLANs in your vSphere infrastructure, you may arrive at a situation where you need to troubleshoot them. This topic will provide you with some tips to obtain and view information about PVLANs and secondary PVLANs, as follows:

1. Log in to the vSphere client and click on **Networking**.
2. Select a distributed switch and right-click on it.
3. From the menu, choose **Edit Settings** and click on it. This will open the **Distributed Switch Settings** window.
4. Click on the third tab named **Private VLAN**.
5. In the section on the left named **Primary private VLAN ID**, verify the VLAN ID provided by your network engineer.
6. You can verify the VLAN ID of the secondary PVLAN in the next section on the right.

Testing virtual machine connectivity

Whenever you are troubleshooting, virtual-machine-to-virtual-machine testing is very important. It helps you to isolate the problem domain to a smaller scope. When performing virtual-machine-to-virtual-machine testing, you should always move virtual machines to a single vSphere host. You can then start troubleshooting the network using basic commands, such as ping. If ping works, you are ready to test it further and move the virtual machines to other hosts, and if it still doesn't work, it most likely is a configuration problem of a physical switch or is likely to be a mismatched physical trunk configuration. The most common problem in this scenario is a problematic physical switch configuration.

Troubleshooting VMkernel interfaces

In this section, we will see how to troubleshoot VMkernel interfaces. A VMkernel interface is a networking interface used in VMware infrastructure for Fault Tolerance, vMotion and IP storage. In vSphere hosts VMkernel interface is responsible for handling vMotion, network connectivity and IP storage. In this section we will see how to troubleshoot VMkernel interfaces using the following commands:

- Confirm VLAN tagging
- Ping to check connectivity
- Vicfg-vmknic

- Escli network ip interface for local configuration

- Escli network ip interface list

- Add or remove

- Set

- Escli network ip interface ipv4 get

You should know how to use these commands to test if everything is working. You should be able to ping to ensure connectivity exists.

We will use the `vicfg-vmknic` command to configure vSphere VMkernel NICs. Let's create a new VMkernel NIC in a vSphere host using the following steps:

1. Log in to your VMware vSphere CLI.

2. Type the following command to create a new VMkernel NIC:

   ```
   vicfg-vmknic –h crimv3esx001.linxsol.com --add --ip 10.2.0.10 –n
   255.255.255.0 'portgroup01'
   ```

You can enable vMotion using the `vicfg-vmknic` command as follows:

`vicfg-vmknic –enable-vmotion.`

You will not be able to enable vMotion from `ESXCLI`. `vMotion` to protect migration of your virtual machines with zero down time.

3. You can delete an existing VMkernel NIC as follows:

   vicfg-vmknic –h crimv3esx001.linxsol.com --delete 'portgroup01'

4. Now check by typing the following command which VMkernel NICs are available in the system:

   vicfg-vmknic -l

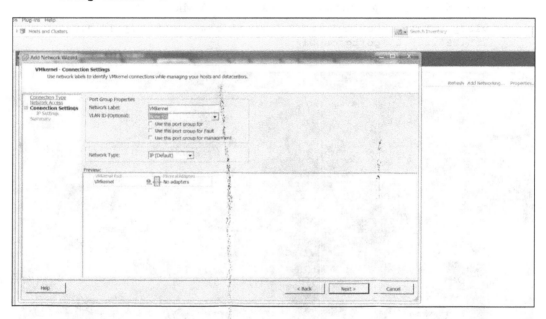

Verifying configuration from DCUI

When you successfully install vSphere, the first yellow screen that you see is called the vSphere DCUI. DCUI is a frontend management system that helps perform some basic system administration tasks. It also offers the best way to troubleshoot some problems that may be difficult to troubleshoot through vMA, vCLI, or PowerCLI. Further, it is very useful when your host becomes irresponsive from the vCenter or is not accessible from any of the management tools.

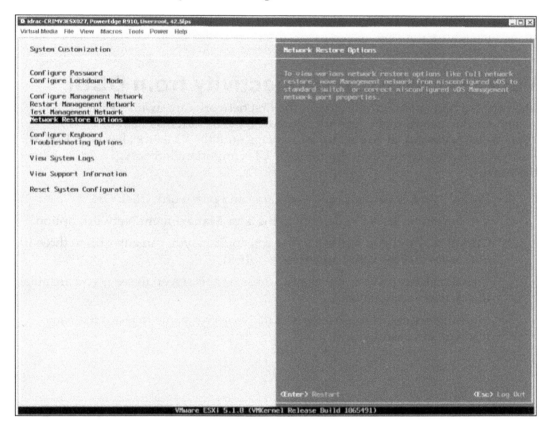

Some useful tasks that can be performed using the DCUI are as follows:

- Configuring the Lockdown mode
- Checking connectivity of the Management Network by Ping
- Configuring and restarting network settings
- Restarting management agents
- Viewing logs
- Resetting vSphere configuration
- Changing the root password

Verifying network connectivity from DCUI

The vSphere host automatically assigns the first network card available to the system for the management network. Moreover, the default installation of the vSphere host does not let you set up VLAN tags until the VMkernel has been loaded. Verifying network connectivity from the DCUI is important but easy. To do so, follow these steps:

1. Press *F2* and enter your root user name and password. Click **OK**.
2. Use the cursor keys to go down to the **Test Management Network** option.
3. Click *Enter,* and you will see a new screen. Here you can enter up to three IP addresses and the host name to be resolved.
4. You can also type your gateway address on this screen to see if you are able to reach to your gateway.
5. In the hostname, you can enter your DNS server name to test if the name resolves successfully.

6. Press **Esc** to get back and **Esc** again to log off from the vSphere DCUI.

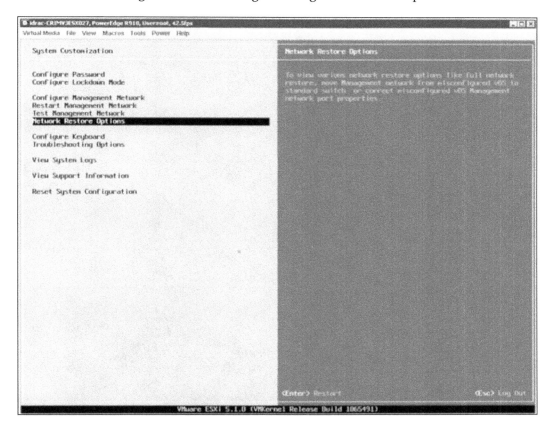

Verifying management network from DCUI

You can also verify the settings of your management network from the DCUI.

1. Press *F2* and enter your root user name and password. Click **OK**.

2. Use the cursor keys to go down to the **Configure Management Network** option and click *Enter*.

3. Click *Enter* again after selecting the first option **Network Adapters**. On the next screen, you will see a list of all the network adapters your system has.

4. It will show you the **Device Name**, **Hardware Type**, **Label**, **Mac Address** of the network card, and the status as **Connected** or **Disconnected**.

5. From the given network cards, you can select or deselect any of the network cards by pressing the spacebar on your keyboard.

6. Press **Esc** to get back and **Esc** again to log off from the vSphere DCUI.

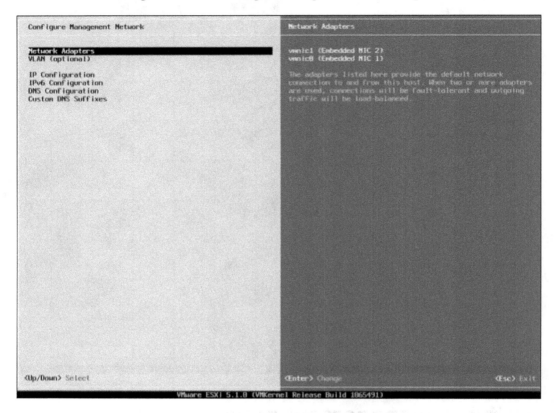

As you can see in the preceding screenshot, you can also configure the IP address and DNS settings for your vSphere host. You can also use DCUI to configure VLANs and DNS Suffix for your vSphere host.

Troubleshooting with port mirroring

Port Mirroring or Switched Port Analyzer is a procedure of analyzing network traffic. As the name suggests, when port mirroring is enabled, you can mirror a copy of network packetes' flow into another port or a VLAN and send it to another port for analysis.

You will see how port mirroring is configured by recognizing a source port and then routing its mirrored traffic to a destination port. Follow this step-by-step guide to enable port mirroring. Right click on a distributed switch and click on **Edit....** Then click on the tab named **Port Mirroring** as seen in the following screenshot:

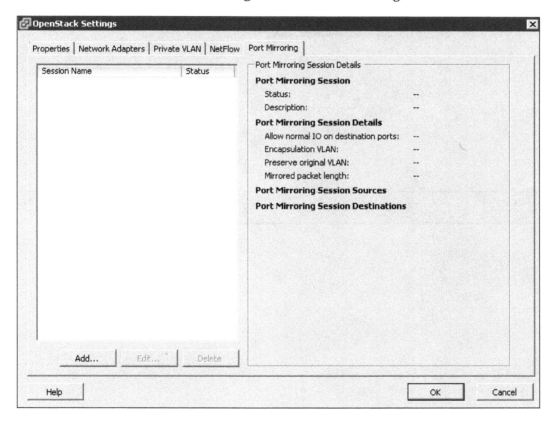

Click on **Add...** as seen in the preceding screenshot. A wizard will appear, where you must specify the **Name** and click **Next**, as you can see in the following screenshot:

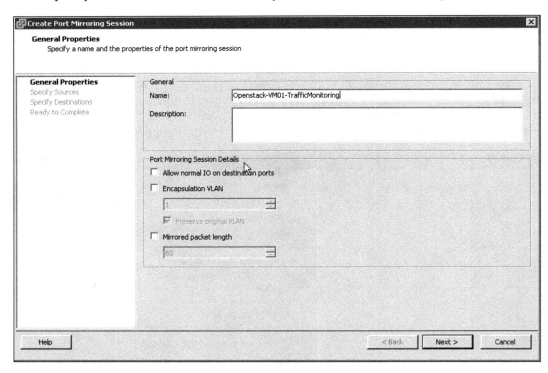

Choose **Ingress** traffic from the **Traffic direction** drop down menu. This menu also includes two other options: **Egress** and **Ingress/Egress**. Define the port number of the virtual machine you want to monitor. You can get the port number from any of the commands that have been discussed previously. In this case, it is **Port ID 110**. Enter it and click **Next**.

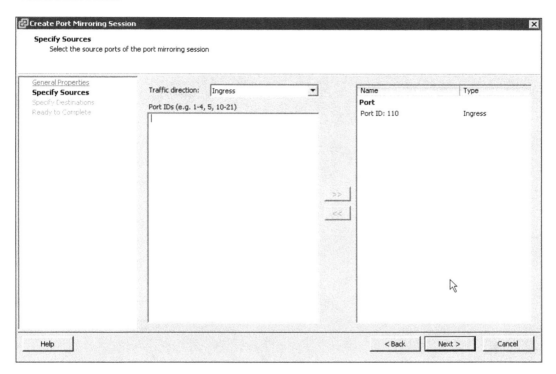

In the next window, you have two options for the **Destination type**: **port** or an **uplink**. You can mirror the traffic to a port, an uplink, or to both, as seen in the following screenshot. Click **Next** once you are done.

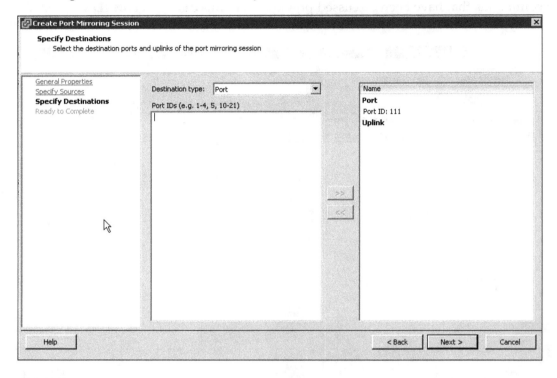

In the following screenshot, you can see a summary of the setting you have chosen. Tick the **Enable this port mirroring session** checkbox to get it in action, and then click on **Finished**.

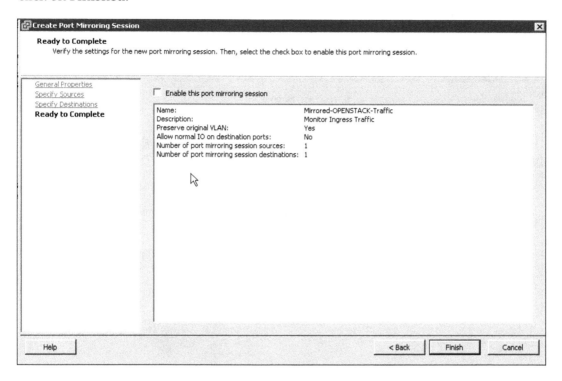

You can see a summary in the following screenshot. As I have not enabled it yet, the status is shown as **Disabled**. Under **Port Mirroring Session Details**, you can see **Preserve original VLAN** is set as **Yes**. Under **Port Mirroring Session Sources** and **Port Mirroring Session Destinations**, you can see **Port ID 110** and **Port ID 111** respectively for the source to capture the traffic from and for the destination traffic is sent to:

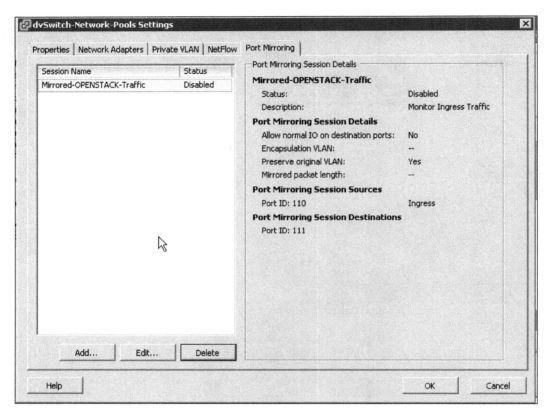

In our virtual infrastructure, we have successfully configured Port Mirroring to troubleshoot and to debug our network issues. This way you can easily analyze ingress, egress, or all the traffic of a port.

Monitoring with NetFlow

You can also use NetFlow to monitor your IP traffic. You can monitor and analyze the network traffic in real time. I am using PRTG to monitor my network, and I will show you how you can configure NetFlow in vSphere to receive this information in PRTG. In vSphere, NetFlow is only supported in vSphere distributed switches, and you require a VMware Enterprise Plus License for it.

1. Go to **Networking** in vSphere. Right-click on a distributed switch and click on **Edit** settings. Then click on the tab named **NetFlow**.

2. Enter the information in the different fields in order to make NetFlow work.

3. Under **Collector Settings**, enter the IP address of your monitoring server. In the **Port** field, enter the port number your monitoring server is listening on.

4. In the VDS IP address field, enter the management IP address for the distributed switch. It is not essential, but I will advise that you enter it. It will help you recognize in your monitoring server the traffic that is coming from the specific IP address.

5. Then click **OK**, and your settings will take effect.

 I will refer you to check the settings of the Network Monitoring system to configure NetFlow accordingly.

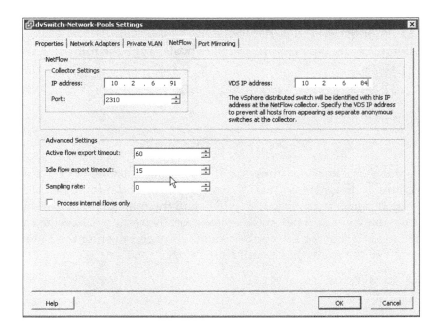

The `vicfg-route` command is very similar to the route command found in Linux. The `vicfg-route` command is very handy to find existing IP gateway settings or to set up your new IP gateway for the ESXi host. To display the default IP gateway, you just need to type the `vicfg-route` command in the terminal. It will display your IPv4 gateway in the CLI. You can use `--family` to display the IPv6 gateway if available:

```
vicfg-route --family v6
```

You can see in the following screenshot that by default, the `vicfg-route` command has displayed the IPv4 gateway. As I do not have the IPv6 default gateway set up, it shows that the IPv6 default gateway is not set:

```
10.2.6.93 - PuTTY                                                    _ □ ✕
vi-admin@vma:~> vifptarget --set crimv3esx001.linxsol.com
vi-admin@vma:~[crimv3esx001.qcri.org]> vicfg-route
Enter username: root
Enter password:
VMkernel IPv4 default gateway is 10.2.6.1
vi-admin@vma:~[crimv3esx001.linxsol.com]> vicfg-route --family v6
Enter username: root
Enter password:
VMkernel IPv6 default gateway is not set
vi-admin@vma:~[crimv3esx001.linxsol.com]>
```

Adding a default route

Let's add a default route in one of the vSphere hosts. Type the following command to add an IPv4 gateway:

```
vicfg-route -a 10.2.0.0/24 10.2.0.254
```

You can also type it this way:

```
vicfg-route -a 10.2.0.0 255.255.255.0 10.2.0.254
```

The command is very simple to understand, the `-a` flag tells the `vicfg-route` command to add an IP gateway route. You can confirm if the route has been added successfully by typing `vicfg-route`. It will list all the relevant networks and their corresponding gateways and net masks. However, the route we have just added is still not the default root for the vSphere host. You need to enter the following command to make the route the default route:

```
vicfg-route -a default 10.2.0.254
```

You can also type the following:

```
vicfg-route 10.2.0.254
```

For IPv6 networks, the command is slightly different:

```
vicfg-route -f V6 -a default 2002:a43:2363:1::1
```

Deleting a route

You can also use the `vicfg-route` command to delete a route or a default route. To delete a route, type the following:

```
vicfg-route -d 10.2.0.0/24 10.2.0.254
```

The `-d` flag tells the `vicfg-route` command to delete the root specified next to it.

Managing vSphere DNS

You can quickly configure, test, and troubleshoot your DNS settings from your vMA appliance. You can always type `--help` with the `vicfg-dns` command to see quick help reference. Log in to your vMA appliance and set the target vSphere host:

```
vifptarget --set crimv3esx001.linxsol.com
```

To view the current DNS setting, simply type the following:

```
vicfg-dns
DNS Configuration


Host Name        crimv3esx001
Domain Name      linxsol.com
DHCP             false
DNS Servers
                 crimv3dns001.linxsol.com
                     crimv3dns002.linxsol.com
```

Let's change the DNS configuration of the vSphere host. Type the following command into your vMA appliance:

```
vicfg-dns -D crimv3dns003.linxsol.com, crimv3dns004.linxsol.com
Updated Host DNS network configuration successfully.
```

Check if the new configuration has been implemented with the following command:

```
vicfg-dns
DNS Configuration

Host Name        crimv3esx001
Domain Name      linxsol.com
DHCP             false
DNS Servers

                 crimv3dns003.linxsol.com
                   crimv3dns004.linxsol.com
```

The following screenshot shows how to set up DNS from the vSphere client:

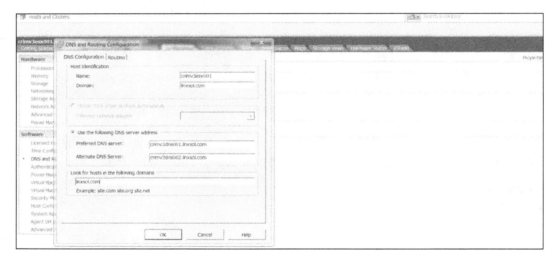

Performing different DNS operations from `esxcli` is not very different from using the `vicfg-dns` command. To list the configured DNS servers from the vSphere host, type the following command in the vSphere console:

```
esxcli network ip dns server list
DNSServers: crimv3dns003.linxsol.com, crimv3dns004.linxsol.com
```

Adding a new DNS server through vSphere CLI:

```
esxcli network ip dns server add -s crimv3dns001.linxsol.com
```

You can use this command repeatedly to add multiple DNS servers. To remove an existing DNS server, use the following command:

```
esxcli network ip dns server remove -s crimv3dns003.linxsol.com
```

You can also configure the search domain for your DNS. I will configure the vSphere host to search locally for http://www.linxsol.com/. Let's first list the already configured search list:

```
esxcli network ip dns search list
DNSSearch Domains:
```

As you can see in the output, nothing has already been configured:

```
esxcli network ip dns search add -d linxsol.com
```

List again the DNS search list:

```
esxcli network ip dns search list
DNSSearch Domains: linxsol.com
```

Let's remove linxsol.com from the search list:

```
esxcli network ip dns search remove -d linxsol.com
```

> Another very important command that you should know when troubleshooting DNS is the one that lists the vSphere hostname. You can use the following command to list the fully qualified hostname for your vSphere host:
>
> ```
> esxcli system hostname get
> Domain Name: linxsol.com
> Fully Qualified Domain Name: crimv3esx001.linxsol.com
> Host Name: crimv3esx001
> ```

PowerCLI - changing DNS on multiple vSphere hosts

Here is a small PowerCLI script to change DNS servers on all the available vSphere hosts in vCenter. Connect your vCenter from the PowerCLI by using `Connect-VIServer`:

```
# DNS Servers to be Added
$dns01 = "crimv3dns001.linxsol.com"
$dns02 = "crimv3dns002.linxsol.com"


# DNS Search Domain
$domainname = "linxsol.com"



$vSphereHosts = get-VMHost


foreach ($vSphere in $vSphereHosts) {

    Write-Host "Updating DNS Configuration of $vSphere" -ForegroundColor
Blue
    Get-VMHostNetwork -VMHost $vSphere | Set-VMHostNetwork -DomainName
$domainname -DNSAddress $dns01, $dns02 -Confirm:$false


}
Write-Host "Successfully completed" -ForegroundColor Green
```

The `dns01` and `dns02` can be replaced with your DNS servers. `Get-VMhost` presents the list of vSphere hosts from the vCenter. Then, we loop the retrieved vSphere hosts one by one to change their DNS settings using `Set-VMHostNetwork -DomainName linxsol.com -DNSAddress crimv3dns01.linxsol.com, crimv3dns02.linxsol.com`. Once it is completed, the script prints **Successfully completed** and exits.

> The preceding PowerCLI script requires two DNS servers. If you have only one DNS server, you can remove `$dns002` from the script.

You can also manually check if the DNS has been updated correctly by typing the following command in PowerCLI 5 or higher:

`Get-VMHostNetwork | Select Hostname, DNSAddress`

```
Vmware vSphere PowerCLI 6.0 Release 1
PowerCLI C:\Program Files (x86)\VMware\Infrastructure\vSphere PowerCLI> Get-VMHost | Get-VMHostNetwork | Select Hostname, DNSAddress

HostName                                                              DnsAddress
--------                                                              ----------
crimv3esx001                                                          crimv3dns001.linxsol.com, crimv3dns002.linxsol.com
crimv3esx002                                                          crimv3dns001.linxsol.com, crimv3dns002.linxsol.com
crimv3esx003                                                          crimv3dns001.linxsol.com, crimv3dns002.linxsol.com
crimv3esx004                                                          crimv3dns001.linxsol.com, crimv3dns002.linxsol.com
crimv3esx005                                                          crimv3dns001.linxsol.com, crimv3dns002.linxsol.com
crimv3esx006                                                          crimv3dns001.linxsol.com, crimv3dns002.linxsol.com
crimv3esx007                                                          crimv3dns001.linxsol.com, crimv3dns002.linxsol.com
crimv3esx008                                                          crimv3dns001.linxsol.com, crimv3dns002.linxsol.com
crimv3esx009                                                          crimv3dns001.linxsol.com, crimv3dns002.linxsol.com
crimv3esx010                                                          crimv3dns001.linxsol.com, crimv3dns002.linxsol.com
crimv3esx011                                                          crimv3dns001.linxsol.com, crimv3dns002.linxsol.com
crimv3esx012                                                          crimv3dns001.linxsol.com, crimv3dns002.linxsol.com
crimv3esx013                                                          crimv3dns001.linxsol.com, crimv3dns002.linxsol.com
crimv3esx014                                                          crimv3dns001.linxsol.com, crimv3dns002.linxsol.com
crimv3esx015                                                          crimv3dns001.linxsol.com, crimv3dns002.linxsol.com
crimv3esx016                                                          crimv3dns001.linxsol.com, crimv3dns002.linxsol.com
crimv3esx017                                                          crimv3dns001.linxsol.com, crimv3dns002.linxsol.com
crimv3esx018                                                          crimv3dns001.linxsol.com, crimv3dns002.linxsol.com
crimv3esx019                                                          crimv3dns001.linxsol.com, crimv3dns002.linxsol.com
crimv3esx020                                                          crimv3dns001.linxsol.com, crimv3dns002.linxsol.com
PowerCLI C:\Program Files (x86)\VMware\Infrastructure\vSphere PowerCLI> _
```

To export the output to CVS format, use the following command:
`Get-VMHostNetwork | Select Hostname, DNSAddress | Export-csv "C:\dns-list.csv"`

Summary

In this chapter, we saw the vSphere log files relevant to networking. We also looked at some of the basic switching concepts. For troubleshooting, we took a deep dive into the troubleshooting commands and some of the monitoring tools to monitor network performance.

The various platforms to execute different commands help you to isolate your troubleshooting techniques. For example, for troubleshooting a single vSphere host, you may like to use `esxcli`, but for a bunch of vSphere hosts you would like to automate scripting tasks from PowerCLI or from a vMA appliance.

In the next chapter, we will look at how to troubleshoot different storage problems in a vSphere infrastructure.

5
Monitoring and Troubleshooting Storage

The VMware vSphere host hides the physical storage layer from end users, and instead, provides a logical storage layer to interact. Virtual machines use virtual disks, which reside on a **VMware Virtual Machine File System** (**VMFS**) datastore. Virtual disks are also stored in raw disk datastores or NFS-based datastores. Virtual machines use virtual SCSI controllers, including VMware Paravirtual, BusLogic Parallel, LSI Logic Parallel, and LSI Logic SAS to access the virtual disks in datastores. We will discuss the following topics in this chapter:

- Storage log files
- Multipathing and **Pluggable Storage Architecture** (**PSA**) troubleshooting
- **Logical unit numbers** (**LUNs**) and claim rules
- Storage module troubleshooting
- Troubleshooting iSCSI datastores
- iSCSI error correction
- Troubleshooting NFS datastores
- Troubleshooting VMFS datastores
- SAN display problems
- SAN performance troubleshooting
- Snapshot and resignaturing

Storage adapters

vSphere hosts use different types of storage adapters. iSCSI, **Fiber Channel (FC)**, **Fiber Channel over Ethernet (FCoE)**, RAID, and Ethernet adapters are supported by vSphere hosts.

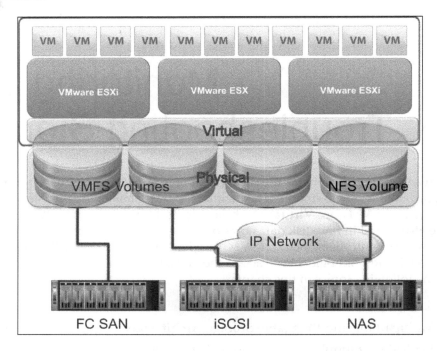

The following table enlists the different types of storage and their compatible adapters (log files that are important to troubleshoot storage issues will be discussed following the table):

Compatible SAN storage for vSphere hosts

Storage Type	Storage Protocols	Data Transfer Type	Interface Type
FC	FC and SCSI	LUN and Block access	FC host bus adapter
FCoE	FCoE and SCSI	LUN and Block access	Converged network adapter (hardware FCoE) and NIC with FCoE (software FCoE)
iSCSI	SCSI and IP	LUN and Block access	iSCSI host bus adapter/iSCSI-enabled hardware NIC and iSCSI-enabled software NIC

Storage log files

We will again start with the logging files as we we did in the previous chapters. The log files always provide a distinctive and systematized way of beginning troubleshooting. For storage issues, the most important vSphere host log files are hostd.log, storageRM.log, and vmkernel.log. We briefly reviewed vSphere hosts and vCenter Server log files in *Chapter 1, The Methodology of Problem Solving*.

The hostd.log file

The hostd.log files contain the logs of virtual machines, different events and tasks of vSphere hosts, vpxa agent, vCenter Server, and vSphere client logs. Logs related to SDK connections are also logged in these files.

The storageRM.log file

Storage I/O Control (SIOC) related problems are logged into /var/log/storagerm. log. You can check this file if SIOC is not working normally or I/O prioritization is not working for virtual machines, as expected in bottlenecks or otherwise. Sometimes you see a message stating Storage I/O control: connection with vobd failed in the /var/log/storagerm.log file. The vSphere host also has a vobd daemon running that logs kernel level errors for monitoring and troubleshooting.

The log entry exists if the vobd daemon is not running. The following screenshot shows the previously mentioned message:

```
# tail /var/log/storagerm.log
014-01-07T12:15:50.364Z: Storage I/O Control: Starting module...
014-01-07T12:15:50.364Z: Running Storage I/O Control at host:   crimv3esx001.linxsol.com
014-07-27T12:57:51.876Z: host Uuid: 526f9e25-4db4-1844-b341-b8ca3af301cd
014-07-27T12:57:51.876Z: Storage I/O Control: connection with vobd failed, error code: -1 errno: 2
014-07-27T12:57:51.877Z: Random Seed: 877333
014-07-27T12:57:51.878Z: Launched injector thread.
014-07-27T12:57:51.878Z: Storage I/O Control: Starting module...
014-07-27T12:57:51.878Z: Running Storage I/O Control at host:   crimv3esx001.linxsol.com
014-07-27T12:57:51.878Z: <<throttled>> Storage I/O Control: connection with vobd failed, error code: -1 errno: 2
014-07-27T12:58:11.884Z: Storage I/O Control: connection with vobd established
# /etc/init.d/vobd status
obd is running
#
#
#
```

As you can see in the preceding screenshot, once the `vobd` service starts running, the connection with the `vobd` established message appears in the `storagerm.log` file. If you are using SIOC on NFS datastores, `storagerm.log` file is a good starting point to troubleshoot any related issues.

The vmkernel.log file

In the `/var/log/vmkernel.log` file, you can find the information about mounting, unmounting, scanning, and rescanning of datastores and storage devices. The `vmkernel.log` file is a very important vSphere host log file for overall host troubleshooting. All the information regarding new LUNs of iSCSI and FCP are also logged in this file. This file is also useful to find any connectivity issues among storage devices. We have already seen in the previous chapter, how to troubleshoot networking issues using `vmkernel.log` file.

DRMDump

All the logging information about the distributed resource scheduler is logged in the following location: `C:\ProgramData\VMware\VMwareVirtualCenter\Logs\drmdump\*.*`.

Multipathing and PSA troubleshooting

PSA is a collection of storage APIs used by a vSphere host using a VMkernel layer. PSA has different components, and its open and modular framework design allows an independent storage design for third-party SAN developers to directly interact with the storage I/O path of vSphere hosts.

PSA manages different plugins that perform different I/O operations, for example, synchronizing the concurrent I/O access, path selection, and load balancing can be defined by **multiple multipathing plugins** (**MPPs**), which can be provided by a SAN provider. The two most famous third-party MPPs are as follows:

- Symantec Dynamic Multi-Pathing (http://goo.gl/dTH2PV)
- EMC PowerPath (http://goo.gl/SNJRXr)

The following screenshot presents PSA and depicts how third-party MPPs are plugged into it:

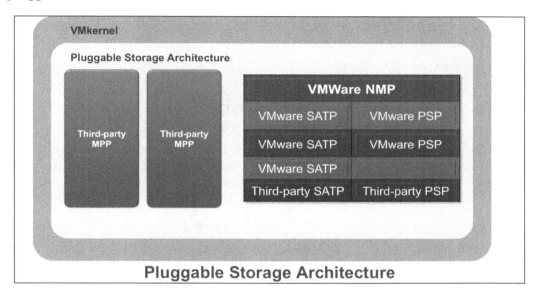

The multipath plugin can publish instructions to the vSphere storage I/O path directly. PSA not only loads and unloads these plugins within VMkernel, it also performs physical path scanning and deletion. PSA directs paths of I/O requests for a logical device to a suitable MPP. It learns storage paths that are available and then decides the assignment of the path ownership to an MPP plugin based on a set of predefined rules. PSA directs the paths of logical devices' I/O requests to a suitable MPP. It manages logical device bandwidth sharing among virtual machines and presents I/O physical path statistics that can be viewed by Performance Charts or esxtop. In physical host bus adapters or in logical adapters, PSA is also responsible for I/O queuing.

After PSA is done handing over the path ownership to the MPP, the MPP manages the physical paths of a LUN or a logical storage device. MPP performs the following functions:

- Claiming physical paths
- Unclaiming physical paths
- Creating, deleting, aborting, or resetting logical devices
- Registering logical devices
- Deregistering logical devices
- Processing I/O requests to logical devices
- Load balancing I/O requests
- Selecting optimal physical paths for I/O requests

Native Multipathing Plugins

VMware also ships a multipath plugin called the VMware **Native Multipathing Plugin** (**NMP**) as part of VMkernel to handle all the storage requests by default within a vSphere host. NMP is also modular in nature and thus manages different sub-plugins to control load balancing and multipathing. NMP has a sub-plugin named **Storage Array Type Plugin** (**SATP**) which performs the following actions:

- Path failover in storage arrays. It monitors path failures and switches the failed path to the available path.
- It supports most of the third-party storage arrays.

Path Selection Plugin (**PSP**) is another subplugin provided by NMP. PSP decides the physical path selection of a load balancing I/O request to a storage array, that includes the following path selection plugins and policies:

- **Fixed – VMW_PSP_FIXED**: If you configure a preferred path for your vSphere host, the PSP algorithm will use it. If a preferred path is not configured, it selects the first discovered available path once the vSphere host boots up. In active-active storage arrays, fixed is the default path selection policy.
- **Round-Robin – VMW_PSP_RR**: PSP applies a Round-Robin algorithm to select the path, and a vSphere host rotates through different active paths. In active-active storage arrays, it utilizes all the available paths, and in active-passive arrays, it uses all the active paths to for I/O requests. To implement load balancing among all the paths for different LUNs, you can use the Round-Robin policy.

- **Most recently Used – VMW_PSP_MRU**: If you select this policy, vSphere host selects the path that has been used most recently. If a path becomes available, vSphere host utilizes it, but it doesn't select the original path once it becomes available again.

 Changing multipath selection policies from a vSphere client will be covered later in this chapter, under the topic *Troubleshooting paths*.

VMware VCLI provides powerful command-line tools to configure multipath plugins. Though there are certain guidelines provided by VMware to configure the plugins, the default SATP, if not already assigned to iSCSI or FC devices, is VMW_SATP_DEFAULT_AA, and the default PSP is VMW_PSP_FIXED.

Refer to the following esxcli storage core claimrule list:

Rule Class	Rule	Class	Type	Plugin	Matches
MP	0	runtime	transport	NMP	transport=usb
MP	1	runtime	transport	NMP	transport=sata
MP	2	runtime	transport	NMP	transport=ide
MP	3	runtime	transport	NMP	transport=block
MP	4	runtime	transport	NMP	transport=unknown
MP	101	runtime	vendor	MASK_PATH	vendor=DELL model=Universal Xport
MP	101	file	vendor	MASK_PATH	vendor=DELL model=Universal Xport
MP	65535	runtime	vendor	NMP	vendor=* model=*

Now let's see what the preceding output means. In the first four lines, NMP claims all the paths. It connects its paths with storage devices that can use the following transport types:

- USB
- SATA
- IDE
- Block SCSI

Using the MASK_PATH module, you can hide your unused storage devices. You can see rule 101 in the preceding output: it is a default PSA claim rule to hide Dell drives.

The category of a claim rule can be determined by the `Rule Class` column. There are three types of categories:

- Multipath plugin
- Filter
- VAAI

From the `Class` column, you can identify which claim rules are being loaded into the system and which claim rules are defined in the system. For example, a claim rule with a class flag of runtime is loaded into the system, but a claim rule with a class flag of file means the claim rule is defined. For the system rules that cannot be modified by you, only the runtime flag exists. When you create a custom claim rule, two lines are added against your rule with the class flags of file and runtime – this means your rule has been defined and is active.

In the last PSA claim rule, notice the `vendor=*` and `model=*` wild card flags. This means all paths to the storage devices that don't match any of the preceding rules should be claimed by NMP.

We can display all the multipath plugins, including those from the third-party plugins, from the VMware vCLI. I will use the plugin list option in VMware vCLI to list all the available plugins. In case the `MASK_PATH` module is active, this will also display that. You can check the available storage plugin list by typing the following command:

```
esxcli storage core plugin list

Plugin name   Plugin class

-----------   ------------

NMP           MP
```

To show a list of the storage devices claimed by NMP, use the `nmp device list` flag as follows:

```
esxcli storage nmp device list

naa.6b8ca3a0f2ab980019ffea2907f89b62
    Device Display Name: Local DELL Disk (naa.6b8ca3a0f2ab980019ffea2907f8
9b62)
    Storage Array Type: VMW_SATP_LOCAL
    Storage Array Type Device Config: SATP VMW_SATP_LOCAL does not support
device configuration.
    Path Selection Policy: VMW_PSP_FIXED
    Path Selection Policy Device Config: {preferred=vmhba0:C2:T0:L0;curren
t=vmhba0:C2:T0:L0}
    Path Selection Policy Device Custom Config:
```

```
    Working Paths: vmhba0:C2:T0:L0
    Is Local SAS Device: false
    Is Boot USB Device: false


naa.6b8ca3a0f2ab980019ffea3b09083f4b
    Device Display Name: Local DELL Disk (naa.6b8ca3a0f2ab980019ffea3b0908
3f4b)
    Storage Array Type: VMW_SATP_LOCAL
    Storage Array Type Device Config: SATP VMW_SATP_LOCAL does not support
device configuration.
    Path Selection Policy: VMW_PSP_FIXED
    Path Selection Policy Device Config: {preferred=vmhba0:C2:T1:L0;curren
t=vmhba0:C2:T1:L0}
    Path Selection Policy Device Custom Config:
    Working Paths: vmhba0:C2:T1:L0
    Is Local SAS Device: false
    Is Boot USB Device: false
```

We can also display NMP SATP information using `nmp satp list` command:

```
esxcli storage nmp satp list
Name                    Default PSP     Description
------------------      -------------   ------------------------------------
-----
VMW_SATP_MSA            VMW_PSP_MRU     Placeholder (plugin not loaded)
VMW_SATP_ALUA           VMW_PSP_MRU     Placeholder (plugin not loaded)
VMW_SATP_DEFAULT_AP     VMW_PSP_MRU     Placeholder (plugin not loaded)
VMW_SATP_SVC            VMW_PSP_FIXED   Placeholder (plugin not loaded)
VMW_SATP_EQL            VMW_PSP_FIXED   Placeholder (plugin not loaded)
VMW_SATP_INV            VMW_PSP_FIXED   Placeholder (plugin not loaded)
VMW_SATP_EVA            VMW_PSP_FIXED   Placeholder (plugin not loaded)
VMW_SATP_ALUA_CX        VMW_PSP_RR      Placeholder (plugin not loaded)
VMW_SATP_SYMM           VMW_PSP_RR      Placeholder (plugin not loaded)
VMW_SATP_CX             VMW_PSP_MRU     Placeholder (plugin not loaded)
VMW_SATP_LSI            VMW_PSP_MRU     Placeholder (plugin not loaded)
VMW_SATP_DEFAULT_AA     VMW_PSP_FIXED   Supports non-specific active/active
arrays
VMW_SATP_LOCAL          VMW_PSP_FIXED   Supports direct attached devices
```

Changing the path selection policy from VMware vMA

We can list the path selection policy by running the following command from the vMA appliance:

```
esxcli storage nmp psp list
Name            Description
------------    --------------------------------
VMW_PSP_MRU     Most Recently Used Path Selection
VMW_PSP_RR      Round Robin Path Selection
VMW_PSP_FIXED   Fixed Path Selection
```

We can list the NMP device list and note down the device number you want to change the path selection policy to:

```
esxcli storage nmp device list
naa.6b8ca3a0f2ab980019ffea2907f89b62
    Device Display Name: Local DELL Disk (naa.6b8ca3a0f2ab980019ffea2907f8
9b62)
    Storage Array Type: VMW_SATP_LOCAL
    Storage Array Type Device Config: SATP VMW_SATP_LOCAL does not support
device configuration.
    Path Selection Policy: VMW_PSP_FIXED
    Path Selection Policy Device Config: {preferred=vmhba0:C2:T0:L0;curren
t=vmhba0:C2:T0:L0}
    Path Selection Policy Device Custom Config:
    Working Paths: vmhba0:C2:T0:L0
    Is Local SAS Device: false
    Is Boot USB Device: false


naa.6b8ca3a0f2ab980019ffea3b09083f4b
    Device Display Name: Local DELL Disk (naa.6b8ca3a0f2ab980019ffea3b0908
3f4b)
    Storage Array Type: VMW_SATP_LOCAL
    Storage Array Type Device Config: SATP VMW_SATP_LOCAL does not support
device configuration.
    Path Selection Policy: VMW_PSP_FIXED
    Path Selection Policy Device Config: {preferred=vmhba0:C2:T1:L0;curren
t=vmhba0:C2:T1:L0}
```

```
Path Selection Policy Device Custom Config:
Working Paths: vmhba0:C2:T1:L0
Is Local SAS Device: false
Is Boot USB Device: false
```

To change the multipath policy, run the following command, replace the device name you have noted down from the preceding command, and then replace the PSP of your choice—you can always use the first command to list all the PSPs:

```
esxcli storage nmp device set --device naa.6b8ca3a0f2ab980019ffea2907f8
9b62 --psp VMW_PSW_FIXED
```

To change the default policy for SATP, execute the following command:

```
esxcli storage nmp satp set --satp VMW_SATP_DEFAULT_AA --default-psp VMW_
PSP_MRU
Default PSP for VMW_SATP_DEFAULT_AA is now VMW_PSP_MRU
```

To list the NMP path for the preceding storage device, execute the following command:

```
esxcli storage nmp path list --device naa.6b8ca3a0f2ab980019ffea2907f8
9b62

unknown.vmhba0-unknown.2:0-naa.6b8ca3a0f2ab980019ffea2907f89b62
    Runtime Name: vmhba0:C2:T0:L0
    Device: naa.6b8ca3a0f2ab980019ffea2907f89b62
    Device Display Name: Local DELL Disk (naa.6b8ca3a0f2ab980019ffea2907f8
9b62)
    Group State: active
    Array Priority: 0
    Storage Array Type Path Config: SATP VMW_SATP_LOCAL does not support
path configuration.
    Path Selection Policy Path Config: {current: yes; preferred: yes}
```

You can identify dead paths using the preceding command. If you see the state as dead in the output of this command, it means a path or paths are down to the storage device. Once identified, you should find more details about the dead path by running the esxcli storage command with the path list flag and the Runtime Name of the device. You will learn how to get the Runtime Name of a storage device later in the chapter. If the path is stated dead again in the following command, you should proceed to check your other hosts to see if they are having the same problem:

```
esxcli storage core path list -p vmhba0:C2:T0:L0
unknown.vmhba0-unknown.2:0-naa.6b8ca3a0f2ab980019ffea2907f89b62
```

```
UID: unknown.vmhba0-unknown.2:0-naa.6b8ca3a0f2ab980019ffea2907f89b62

Runtime Name: vmhba0:C2:T0:L0

Device: naa.6b8ca3a0f2ab980019ffea2907f89b62

Device Display Name: Local DELL Disk (naa.6b8ca3a0f2ab980019ffea2907f8
9b62)

Adapter: vmhba0

Channel: 2

Target: 0

LUN: 0

Plugin: NMP

State: Dead

Transport: parallel

Adapter Identifier: unknown.vmhba0

Target Identifier: unknown.2:0

Adapter Transport Details: Unavailable or path is unclaimed

Target Transport Details: Unavailable or path is unclaimed
```

Storage path masking

We have discussed MASK_PATH in the previous section and seen how it can be used to block a path from a vSphere host to a storage device. When troubleshooting storage paths, the need to mask a storage path may arise due to one of the following situations:

- Blocking vSphere host access to a storage device or a LUN
- Blocking a single path or all paths to a storage device or to a LUN
- Blocking vSphere host to use a particular storage path
- Blocking a whole storage array
- Managing **All Paths Down** (APD) situation (this will be discussed in the next section)

I will demonstrate how a path can be masked from the VMware vCLI later in the chapter.

 The esxcli storage namespace has a lot of useful utility and troubleshooting commands. For a detailed reference, check the VMware documentation (https://goo.gl/4ebE4r).

Some important commands are listed in the following table:

vCLI Storage Namespace	Role
core	For PSA operations, MPP, claim rules
Nfs	For NFS operations, mount, unmount, and listing of NFS datastores
nmp	For NMP, SATP, and PSP operations
vmfs	For VMFS volumes, extents, snapshots, and upgrade operations

LUN and claim rules

To identify disk volumes in a storage array, a LUN is used. For simplicity, LUN is a logical volume that acts for a disk volume on SAN called target. LUNs can be single or in multiples for a single given disk volume or target, depending on the storage provider and the storage configuration for vSphere hosts. LUNs are represented by an integer assigned by a storage array. A single vSphere host can have up to 256 SCSI storage devices or LUNs starting from zero to 255 in older vSphere hosts. Starting from vSphere 6.0, a host can have 1,024 SCSI storage devices ranging from zero to 1,023. While targets are represented by unique names, for example, iSCSI names are used for iSCSI targets and **World Wide Names** (**WWN**) are used for FC.

You can configure the maximum LUN ID in the **Advanced Settings** by changing **Disk.MaxLUN**. In earlier vSphere hosts, it was set to 256 by default, and in vSphere 6.0, to 1024.

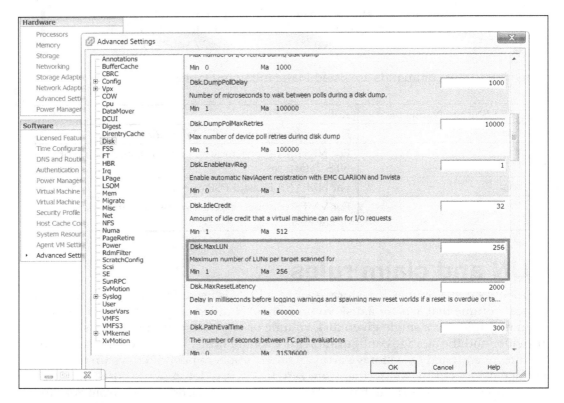

To configure **Disk.MaxLUN**, follow this procedure:

1. Go to **Advanced System Settings** of your vSphere host.
2. Click on **Disk** in the left pane.
3. Scroll down to **Disk.MaxLUN** and change the settings accordingly.

The same LUN cannot be accessed from a fiber channel or iSCSI or any other storage transport protocol, as it is not supported by vSphere hosts.

Be aware that a LUN after 255 can never be discovered by a vSphere host earlier than version 6.0. From vSphere 6.0, the host will not be able to scan after 1,023 SCSI devices.

Identifying storage devices and LUNs

The vSphere host storage troubleshooting requires you to use vSphere command-line utilities to detect a particular disk correctly. Part of troubleshooting also requires your skills to correctly identify connected LUNs to vSphere hosts. Let's view some commands that can be handy in your toolbox to identify the connected disks correctly:

```
esxcli storage core device list
naa.6b8ca3a0f2ab980019ffea2907f89b62
    Display Name: Local DELL Disk (naa.6b8ca3a0f2ab980019ffea2907f89b62)
    Has Settable Display Name: true
    Size: 190208
    Device Type: Direct-Access
    Multipath Plugin: NMP
    Devfs Path: /vmfs/devices/disks/naa.6b8ca3a0f2ab980019ffea2907f89b62
    Vendor: DELL
    Model: PERC H710P
    Revision: 3.13
    SCSI Level: 5
    Is Pseudo: false
    Status: on
    Is RDM Capable: false
    Is Local: true
    Is Removable: false
    Is SSD: false
    Is Offline: false
    Is Perennially Reserved: false
    Queue Full Sample Size: 0
    Queue Full Threshold: 0
    Thin Provisioning Status: unknown
    Attached Filters:
    VAAI Status: unsupported
    Other UIDs: vml.02000000006b8ca3a0f2ab980019ffea2907f89b62504552432048
    Is Local SAS Device: false
    Is Boot USB Device: false
naa.6b8ca3a0f2ab980019ffea3b09083f4b
    Display Name: Local DELL Disk (naa.6b8ca3a0f2ab980019ffea3b09083f4b)
```

```
  Has Settable Display Name: true

  Size: 8008448

  Device Type: Direct-Access

  Multipath Plugin: NMP

  Devfs Path: /vmfs/devices/disks/naa.6b8ca3a0f2ab980019ffea3b09083f4b

  Vendor: DELL

  Model: PERC H710P

  Revision: 3.13

  SCSI Level: 5

  Is Pseudo: false

  Status: on

  Is RDM Capable: false

  Is Local: true

  Is Removable: false

  Is SSD: false

  Is Offline: false

  Is Perennially Reserved: false

  Queue Full Sample Size: 0

  Queue Full Threshold: 0

  Thin Provisioning Status: unknown

  Attached Filters:

  VAAI Status: unsupported

  Other UIDs: vml.02000000006b8ca3a0f2ab980019ffea3b09083f4b504552432048

  Is Local SAS Device: false

  Is Boot USB Device: false

--- Output Omitted ---
```

Here's a brief explanation of the preceding command and its output:

- The preceding command has listed two devices connected to the vSphere hosts.

- In the first line starting with naa, you can see in the output the Device Name with the identifier for the device (also see the following screenshot). Here naa refers to **Network Addressing Authority Identifier**; it is always unique to the device and remains the same all across the vSphere hosts.

- The `Runtime Name` device is missing in the output of the preceding command, but you can also find it from the vSphere client (see the following screenshot) or by using the upcoming command. This name is produced by a vSphere host to indicate the first path to the storage device. You can identify the name of the physical storage adapter on the vSphere host, and channel it to the storage device, target and LUN information.

- The second line shows the `Display Name` of the device. For example, in the screenshot that follows, `vmhba0:C2:T0:L0` signifies there is 0 LUN on target 0 using the storage adapter vmhba0 and channel 2.

- You can see the size of the drive, which has a capacity of about 180 GB, while the second disk has a size of 8 TB.

- The device type is `Direct Access` and the multipath plugin is NMP (we will discuss the multipath plugin later in the chapter). Device type could be a CD-ROM, a local disk, or a network drive. As you can see, other information is also listed, which can be quite useful when troubleshooting.

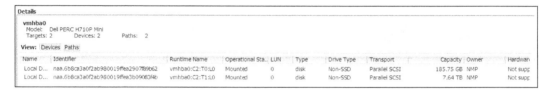

Runtime Name is not persistent and is therefore not a reliable identifier as the **universally unique identifier (UUID)**.

To display information more relevant to one of the devices listed in the preceding output, use the following command in your vSphere host CLI:

```
esxcli storage core path list --device naa.6b8ca3a0f2ab980019ffea3b09083
f4b

unknown.vmhba0-unknown.2:1-naa.6b8ca3a0f2ab980019ffea3b09083f4b
    UID: unknown.vmhba0-unknown.2:1-naa.6b8ca3a0f2ab980019ffea3b09083f4b
    Runtime Name: vmhba0:C2:T1:L0
    Device: naa.6b8ca3a0f2ab980019ffea3b09083f4b
    Device Display Name: Local DELL Disk (naa.6b8ca3a0f2ab980019ffea3b0908
3f4b)
    Adapter: vmhba0
    Channel: 2
    Target: 1
```

```
LUN: 0
Plugin: NMP
State: active
Transport: parallel
Adapter Identifier: unknown.vmhba0
Target Identifier: unknown.2:1
Adapter Transport Details: Unavailable or path is unclaimed
Target Transport Details: Unavailable or path is unclaimed
Maximum IO Size: 286720
```

As you can see, I have used the device name returned by the `esxcli storage core device list` command. The `-d` or `--device` flag in the preceding command represents a device. You can replace the device name according to the particular storage device you are troubleshooting after the `-d` flag. In this command, you can see in the output that the local storage device has zero LUN, 1 target, and 2 channels.

You can see toward the end of the preceding output a message saying `Unavailable or path is unclaimed`. You can troubleshoot claiming the path using the following command:

```
esxcli storage core claiming reclaim  --device naa.6b8ca3a0f2ab980019ffea
3b09083f4b
```

The command will try to unclaim all the paths to the drive at first and then reclaim the paths by running claim rules for each unclaimed path.

For a systematic flowchart for storage troubleshooting, read this VMware **Knowledge Base** article at `http://goo.gl/wBj6fQ`.

You can also display the information about storage adapters using the following command:

```
esxcli storage core adapter list
HBA Name  Driver        Link State   UID             Description
--------  ------------  ----------   --------------  ---------------------
---------------------------------

vmhba0    megaraid_sas  link-n/a     unknown.vmhba0  (0:2:0.0) LSI /
Symbios Logic Dell PERC H710P Mini
vmhba32   iscsi_vmk     online       iscsi.vmhba32   iSCSI Software
Adapter
```

Listing storage devices from vMA

While the process is slightly different, the same information can also be obtained from VMware vMA appliance by using the following commands — this time you do not need to specify a device name, as the command will list all the available devices for a particular vSphere host:

1. Set up your target vSphere host:

   ```
   vi-admin@vma:~> vifptarget --set crimv3esx001.linxsol.com
   ```

2. Use the `vicfg-mpath` command to list the available storage devices:

   ```
   vi-admin@vma:~[crimv3esx001.linxsol.com]> vicfg-mpath -l

   unknown.vmhba0-unknown.2:0-naa.6b8ca3a0f2ab980019ffea2907f89b62
       Runtime Name: vmhba0:C2:T0:L0
       Device: naa.6b8ca3a0f2ab980019ffea2907f89b62
       Device Display Name: Local DELL Disk (naa.6b8ca3a0f2ab980019ffe
   a2907f89b62)
       Adapter: vmhba0 Channel: 2 Target: 0 LUN: 0
       Adapter Identifier: unknown.vmhba0
       Target Identifier: unknown.2:0
       Plugin: NMP
       State: active
       Transport: parallel


   unknown.vmhba0-unknown.2:1-naa.6b8ca3a0f2ab980019ffea3b09083f4b
       Runtime Name: vmhba0:C2:T1:L0
       Device: naa.6b8ca3a0f2ab980019ffea3b09083f4b
       Device Display Name: Local DELL Disk (naa.6b8ca3a0f2ab980019ffe
   a3b09083f4b)
       Adapter: vmhba0 Channel: 2 Target: 1 LUN: 0
       Adapter Identifier: unknown.vmhba0
       Target Identifier: unknown.2:1
       Plugin: NMP
       State: active
       Transport: parallel
   ```

3. You may also need to produce a list of mapping from device name to UUIDs and extents for each volume. Here, you can see the VMFS UUID and the Device Name IDs:

```
esxcli storage vmfs extent list

Volume Name      VMFS UUID                                    Extent Number
Device Name                                    Partition

-------------    ----------------------------------    -------------
----------------------------------    ---------

exx002-123       526fe8a4-a4898996-1b9d-b8ca3af0b2d9                      0
naa.6b8ca3a0f2ab980019ffea2907f89b62          3

esx001-scratch   52726634-c883703c-68b7-b8ca3af0b2d9                      0
naa.6b8ca3a0f2ab980019ffea3b09083f4b          1
```

4. However, the preceding command still does not list the network volumes available to the vSphere host. In case you are troubleshooting a network volume instead of a local volume, this command is not much of a use.

5. To list all the filesystems available to a particular vSphere host, the esxcli storage filesystem list command is available. Here is the output:

```
esxcli storage filesystem list
```

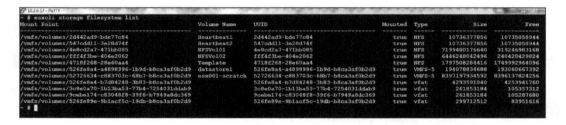

6. Here you can see the volumes available to vSphere host, where it is mounted, the volume name, UUID, mount status, filesystem type, total size, and available capacity.

7. One last thing we will discuss is how to identify the disk or LUN partitions. I will use the ls command to list /vmfs/devices/disks to list all the available disks:

```
ls -alh /vmfs/devices/disks

-rw-------    1 root     root       185.8G Jul 16 12:30 naa.6b8ca3a
0f2ab980019ffea2907f89b62

-rw-------    1 root     root       4.0M Jul 16 12:30 naa.6b8ca3a
0f2ab980019ffea2907f89b62:1

-rw-------    1 root     root       4.0G Jul 16 12:30 naa.6b8ca3a
0f2ab980019ffea2907f89b62:2
```

```
-rw-------      1 root       root        180.9G Jul 16 12:30 naa.6b8ca3a
0f2ab980019ffea2907f89b62:3

-rw-------      1 root       root        250.0M Jul 16 12:30 naa.6b8ca3a
0f2ab980019ffea2907f89b62:5

-rw-------      1 root       root        250.0M Jul 16 12:30 naa.6b8ca3a
0f2ab980019ffea2907f89b62:6

-rw-------      1 root       root        110.0M Jul 16 12:30 naa.6b8ca3a
0f2ab980019ffea2907f89b62:7

-rw-------      1 root       root        286.0M Jul 16 12:30 naa.6b8ca3a
0f2ab980019ffea2907f89b62:8

-rw-------      1 root       root          7.6T Jul 16 12:30 naa.6b8ca3a
0f2ab980019ffea3b09083f4b

-rw-------      1 root       root          7.6T Jul 16 12:30 naa.6b8ca3a
0f2ab980019ffea3b09083f4b:1

--- Omitted Output ---
```

8. The command will also display all the possible targets for particular storage functions. The last number in UUID after the colon is a partition number. You can see that the local disk has 185 GB of space in total with 8 partitions. The second local disk has a size of 7.6 TB and has a single partition. In UUID, the entire disk is represented by a zero after a colon. When performing different operations with VMKFSTOOLS, this command is very handy.

9. You can also use VML Identifier (VML is a legacy identifier) instead of NAA Identifier. VML Identifier can also be used with VMKFSTOOLS. You can find out the VML ID as follows: `vmkfstools -q disk.vmdk`.

10. You can use the `esxcli` command to obtain information about storage statistics. It can also be very helpful to find issues with your vSphere storage infrastructure. You should pay close attention to the metrics starting with `Failed` at the end of the output. You can see in the output `Failed Commands` listed in bold has a very high rate of errors and definitely points to a connection or a storage device issue.

```
esxcli storage core device stats get
naa.6b8ca3a0f2ab980019ffea2907f89b62
    Device: naa.6b8ca3a0f2ab980019ffea2907f89b62
    Successful Commands: 48602249
    Blocks Read: 1800303524
    Blocks Written: 1629033003
    Read Operations: 28763933
    Write Operations: 19457147
    Reserve Operations: 108369
```

```
Reservation Conflicts: 0
Failed Commands: 139227
Failed Blocks Read: 0
Failed Blocks Written: 0
Failed Read Operations: 0
Failed Write Operations: 0
Failed Reserve Operations: 0
```

Troubleshooting paths

LUNs masking can be used to troubleshoot a storage device. To troubleshoot, you can disable storage paths temporarily for a particular vSphere host. This can save you a lot of time during troubleshooting of storage issues.

A vSphere host can declare two states about a storage device loss: **All Paths Down (APD)** or **Permanent Device Loss (PDL)**. An APD signal is triggered when a storage device loses communication with a vSphere host. In this case, a vSphere host believes that the path will be restored shortly and the storage device will be reconnected.

A PDL signal is triggered once a vSphere host identifies that the I/O cannot be queued for the storage device anymore. Once the device is declared to be in a state of permanent loss, the vSphere host doesn't expect it to come back. SCSI sense codes are used by storage devices to communicate with a vSphere host so it can declare a storage device in the path's loss state and specify whether the path's losses are in the state of APD or PDL. For example, to inform about Permanent Device Loss state a storage device logs in VMkernel log file a SCSI sense code of something like this `H:0x0 D:0x2 P:0x0 Valid sense data: 0x5 0x25 0x0` or `Logical Unit Not Supported`. The vSphere host identifies from this SCSI sense code that the storage device lost is permanent and then declares the storage device in a PDL state. In this case, the vSphere host will not try to re-establish a connection with the storage device. If no SCSI sense codes are logged, the vSphere host continues to re-establish a connection with the storage device and considers the device to be in an APD state.

Storage array that doesn't support SCSI sense codes or a device that doesn't generate an SCSI code is declared to be in an APD state as well. The vSphere host keeps trying to send I/O requests until it receives a response.

Disabling vSphere APD

APD handling is enabled by default in vSphere hosts. Since a vSphere host keeps trying to send I/O commands to a storage device, after the time period expires, the host stops sending requests and stops nonvirtual machine I/O. This feature can be disabled so that the vSphere host can try continuously for an unlimited period of time. Disabling APD management can be I/O expensive and your virtual machines can be unresponsive because of I/O timeouts. A good use case to disable APD is when your storage array has one-to-one mapping for a single LUN per target:

1. Login to your vSphere client and click on the **Configuration** tab.
2. From the **Software** pane on the left, select **Advanced Settings**.
3. In **Advanced Settings**, click on **Misc**.
4. Change **Misc.APDHandlingEnable** from 1 to 0 to disable it.
5. You can also increase the APD request timeout settings just below the **Misc. APDHandlingEnable** setting, as seen in the following screenshot:

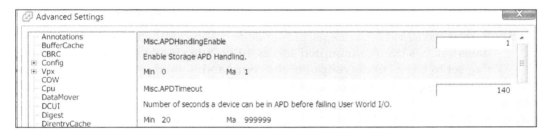

Planned PDL

When you attempt to remove a storage device from a vSphere host, a planned PDL is triggered. Before detaching, make sure you meet the following guidelines:

- Unmount the datastore (using vMA, as described in the upcoming section)
- Detach the device and LUN information before removing it from the storage array
- Move all the virtual machines and other objects before unmounting
- Make sure the datastore is not part of a datastore cluster and is not part of vSphere HA heartbeat
- Disable the Storage DRS, if it is managed by Storage DRS
- Disable Storage I/O Control

For PDL, follow these steps:

1. Obtain the VMFS UUID and the device name IDs using the following command:

   ```
   esxcli storage vmfs extent list
   ```

2. Use `esxcli storage filesystem list` command. This command will list all the VMFS datastores mounted to a vSphere host.:

   ```
   esxcli storage filesystem list
   ```

3. Run the following command to produce a list of VMFS datastore volumes and their UUIDs, if not already produced in step 1:

   ```
   esxcfg-scsidevs -m
   ```

4. Unmount the datastore using the following command:

   ```
   esxcli storage filesystem unmount -1 esx001-scratch
   ```

   This command will unmount the `esx001-scratch` datastore from the vSphere host.

5. Repeat the `esxcli storage filesystem list` command to verify if the datastore has been unmounted successfully. You should see the mounted flag set to `false` in the output of the command:

   ```
   esxcli storage filesystem list
   ```

6. Detach the device or LUN — you will see in the output the status of the disk is off:

   ```
   esxcli storage core device list -d naa.6b8ca3a0f2ab980019ffea3b090
   83f4b
   ```

7. Verify that the device has been successfully detached by running `partedUtil`:

   ```
   partedUtil getptbl /vmfs/devices/disks/naa.6b8ca3a0f2ab980019ffea3
   b09083f4b
   ```

   This command should return the `device is not found` message.

8. Remove the LUN from the SAN.

9. Rescan your devices. Replace the adapter name with your adapter in the following command:

```
esxcli storage core adapter rescan -A vmhba0
```

10. To remove the entries from the vSphere host configuration, first list the entries and make note of the entries that are in the off state:

```
esxcli storeage core device detached list
```

11. Remove the device configuration entries permanently from the vSphere host:

```
esxcli storage core device detached remove -d naa.6b8ca3a0f2ab9800
19ffea3b09083f4b
```

VMware vMA to automate detaching of LUNs

The procedure described in the preceding section is good if you want to detach LUNs from a single vSphere host. But what if you have a hundred vSphere hosts and you need to detach from all of them in a short time? Obviously you need to automate the process. This can be achieved using vSphere PowerCLI as well as vMA:

1. Download the VMware community supported PERL script from in your vMA appliance from the following URL using `wget`:

```
wget -no-check-certificate https://raw.githubusercontent.com/lamw/
vghetto-scripts/master/perl/lunManagement.pl
```

2. Make it executeable:

```
chmod +x lunManagement.pl
```

3. Run the script from your vMA appliance and list all the datastores available using vCenter authentication; the command will also show you the status of the datastores if they are mounted and attached (as seen in the following screenshot):

```
./lunManagement.pl --server vcs001.linxsol.com --username linxsol.
com\zeeshan --operation list
```

4. Unmount the datastore using the following command:

```
./lunManagement.pl --server vcs001.linsol.com --username linxsol.
com\zeeshan --operation unmount --datastore esx001-scratch
```

5. Verify that the datastore `esx001-scratch` has been successfully unmounted:

```
./lunManagement.pl --server vcs001.linsol.com --username linxsol.
com\zeeshan --operation list
```

6. Detach the datastore `esx001-scratch` by running the following command:

```
./lunManagement.pl --server vcs001.linsol.com --username linxsol.
com\zeeshan --operation detach --datastore esx001-scratch
```

7. Verify if the detachment is successful:

```
./lunManagement.pl --server vcs001.linsol.com --username linxsol.
com\zeeshan --operation list
```

Unplanned PDL

We have seen PDL and some useful tips to manage it successfully. Sometimes you come across an unplanned PDL when your vSphere host loses connectivity permanently to a storage device. Sometimes an unplanned device loss occurs and your vSphere host loses connectivity permanently to a storage device. By using SCSI sense codes, as mentioned earlier, a vSphere host is able to identify if the storage device is in a permanent loss state. The vSphere host then marks that storage device as not attached and logs a warning message of the storage device not being available permanently in the `/var/log/VMkernel.log` file.

Usually, unplanned device loss happens because of some hardware problem that is not recoverable or when the LUN ID changes. Network disconnection can also cause unplanned device loss. When troubleshooting an unplanned device loss state, follow these steps:

1. Remove the persistent information linked with the device.

2. Verify the status of the device, for example, network connectivity and LUN ID match.

3. Switch off and unregister all virtual machines affected by unplanned PDL.

4. Unmount any associated datastores using the procedure described in previous section.

5. Perform a storage rescan on all vSphere hosts that were accessing the storage device.

Multipath policy selection from the vSphere client

You can also identify multipath policy selection settings from the vSphere client. For the sake of completeness, you should be able to obtain multipath information from the vSphere client. For that perform the following steps:

1. Log in to your vSphere client.

2. Click on the vSphere host named **crimv3esx001.linxsol.com** and go to the **Configuration** tab.

3. Click on **Storage** in the **Hardware** pane on the left.

4. Select the datastore you want to display the multipath settings in and right-click on it.

5. Choose **Properties** from the menu to open the **Properties** window of the datastore.

6. From **Extents**, select a device and click on **Manage Paths**. You can see the available paths for the datastore.

You can change the multipath information here to the policy of your choice.

Using vMA to change a path state

A path state can be changed from `esxcli` and from a VMware vMA appliance. This procedure will not work if an active I/O operation is going on. If the command fails, wait for some time so that the I/O operation can be finished first:

1. Log in to your vMA appliance and set up your target vSphere host:

   vi-admin@vma:~> vifptarget --set crimv3esx001.linxsol.com

2. Use the `vicfg-mpath` command to list the available storage devices:

   vi-admin@vma:~[crimv3esx001.linxsol.com]> vicfg-mpath -l

3. From the output of the preceding command, note down the `Runtime Name`. The `Runtime Name` information will be used in the next command to turn off the path state:

   vi-admin@vma:~[crimv3esx001.linxsol.com]> vicfg-mpath --state off --path vmhba0:C2:T1:L0

4. To re-activate the path into its original state, use the following command:

```
vi-admin@vma:~[crimv3esx001.linxsol.com]> vicfg-mpath --state
active --path vmhba0:C2:T1:L0
```

5. Mask the path with MASK_PATH. Log in to your vMA appliance and set up your target vSphere host:

```
vi-admin@vma:~> vifptarget --set crimv3esx001.linxsol.com
```

6. List the available storage devices to make sure the devices are available to the vSphere host and write down the Runtime Name you want to mask a path:

```
vi-admin@vma:~[crimv3esx001.linxsol.com]> vicfg-mpath -l
```

7. Add the mask rule as follows for the DELL storage device:

```
esxcli storage core claimrule add -r 101 -t vendor --vendor=DELL
--model='Universal Xport' -A vmhba0 -C 2 -L 1 -P MASK_PATH
```

8. Load the the recently added rule by running the following command:

```
esxcli storage core claimrule load
```

9. List the claim rules:

```
esxcli storage core claimrule list
```

Unmasking a path

For unmasking a path, perform the following steps:

1. Log in to your vMA appliance and set up your target vSphere host:

    `vi-admin@vma:~> vifptarget --set crimv3esx001.linxsol.com`

2. List the claim rules and note the number of the rules you want to delete:

    `esxcli storage core claimrule list`

3. I will delete the recently added `rule 101`:

    `esxcli storage core claimrule remove --rule 101`

4. Load the the recently added rule by running the following command:

    `esxcli storage core claimrule load`

5. List the claim rules to verify the rule has been deleted successfully:

    `esxcli storage core claimrule list`

```
10.2.6.93 - PuTTY
vi-admin@vma:~[crimv3esx001.qcri.org]> esxcli storage core claimrule list
Rule Class  Rule   Class    Type       Plugin    Matches
----------  -----  -------  ---------  ------    ------------------
MP              0  runtime  transport  NMP          transport=usb
MP              1  runtime  transport  NMP          transport=sata
MP              2  runtime  transport  NMP          transport=ide
MP              3  runtime  transport  NMP          transport=block
MP              4  runtime  transport  NMP          transport=unknown
MP            101  runtime  vendor     MASK_PATH    vendor=DELL model=Universal Xport
MP            101  file     vendor     MASK_PATH    vendor=DELL model=Universal Xport
MP          65535  runtime  vendor     NMP          vendor=* model=*
vi-admin@vma:~[crimv3esx001.qcri.org]> esxcli storage core claimrule remove --rule 101
vi-admin@vma:~[crimv3esx001.qcri.org]> esxcli storage core claimrule load
vi-admin@vma:~[crimv3esx001.qcri.org]> esxcli storage core claimrule list
Rule Class  Rule   Class    Type       Plugin    Matches
----------  -----  -------  ---------  ------    ------------------
MP              0  runtime  transport  NMP          transport=usb
MP              1  runtime  transport  NMP          transport=sata
MP              2  runtime  transport  NMP          transport=ide
MP              3  runtime  transport  NMP          transport=block
MP              4  runtime  transport  NMP          transport=unknown
MP          65535  runtime  vendor     NMP          vendor=* model=*
vi-admin@vma:~[crimv3esx001.qcri.org]>
```

LUN troubleshooting tips

Sometimes LUNs are not visible in vCenter or in your vSphere hosts or you are unable to connect to the SAN. You can use the following tips in such situations:

- Always verify the settings in your SAN that is publishing the LUN.

- Make sure LUNs exist on the same storage network where your vSphere hosts can reach.

- LUNs should be readable and writeable by your vSphere hosts.

- As previously described, Host ID on the LUN should be less than 1,023 in vSphere hosts 6.0, and less than 255 in vSphere hosts 5.0. The vSphere hosts will not be able to scan higher LUN IDs even if they exist on the SAN.

- Make sure the LUNs are configured correctly in your SAN as well as in the vSphere hosts.

- From vSphere hosts, verify the LUN information using the VCLI `esxcli storage core path list` command and r `vicfg-mpath -l` command from the vMA appliance.

Latency is a well-known problem that can occur if your vSphere infrastructure is not set up correctly. As described in previous chapters, use esxtop to verify any storage latency issues.

Storage module troubleshooting

All the storage-related APIs communicate with VMkernel through storage modules. You should know some of the basic commands for troubleshooting VMkernel storage module issues.

To list all the storage modules, use the following command, which will also display the modules that are loaded within VMkernel and the status of each module—whether it is enabled or not in the active state:

```
esxcli system module list
Name                             Is Loaded  Is Enabled
-----------------------------    ---------  ----------
vmkernel                         true       true
chardevs                         true       true
user                             true       true
vmkapei                          true       true
dell                             true       true
vprobe                           true       true
```

procfs	true	true
procMisc	true	true
vmkapi_socket	true	true
vmkapi_v2_0_0_0_vmkernel_shim	true	true
vmkplexer	true	true
vmklinux_9	true	true
vmklinux_9_2_0_0	true	true
vmklinux_9_2_1_0	true	true
random	true	true
usb	true	true
ehci-hcd	true	true
hid	true	true
ipmi_msghandler	true	true
ipmi_si_drv	true	true
ipmi_devintf	true	true
iscsi_trans	true	true
etherswitch	true	true

You can get information about the parameters of a certain module. The following command will display available parameters for a module named `nfsclient`: its parameter name, value, and description. The name of the parameter in the output of the following command is `oneRequest` and its type is `Boolean`:

```
esxcli system module parameters list --module nfsclient
Name        Type  Value  Description
----------  ----  -----  ------------------------------------------------
------------
oneRequest  bool         Only allow one outsanding request at a time
(debugging only)
```

Troubleshooting iSCSI-related issues

The vSphere hosts also use IP-based storage as a remote storage. VCLI provides powerful command-line tools to monitor, manage, and troubleshoot IP storage. Two namespaces are provided by VMware—`esxcli iscsi` and `vicfg-iscsi`—to perform the different configuration of iSCSI storage and vSphere hosts.

The vSphere hosts use two different processes to discover iSCSI targets: dynamic discovery and static discovery. In the dynamic discovery process, all targets are discovered by the iSCSI target name and the IP address or a hostname. In the static discovery process, you need to configure a hostname or IP address and an iSCSI target name manually. iSCSI target names are similar to UUID to identify iSCSI targets. It could be an IQN or EUI name as can be seen in the following screenshot:

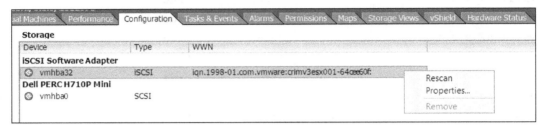

You can see the IQN name has the year `1998` and month `01` as part of the name which is the domain registration date. The next part `com.vmware:crimv3esx001` is a reversed domain name, and the last part is a unique identity string.

Follow these guidelines to troubleshoot iSCSI storage issues:

- All iSCSI related errors are logged in `/var/log/syslog.log` by default. This file could be a good starting point for troubleshooting.

- Always make sure that the iSCSI target device is listening to iSCSI connections. The default TCP port for the iSCSI server is 3260. If there are any firewalls involved between your storage infrastructure and vSphere infrastructure, make sure to add an exception rule for TCP port 3260 in your firewall. You can use the `telnet` utility to verify if the port is an open or closed state:

```
telnet storage001.linxsol.com 3260
```

- You can also use a Powershell script to find if the port is accessible:

```
[CmdletBinding()]

Param(

  [Parameter(Mandatory=$True,Position=1)]

  [string]$StorageSrvAdd,
```

```
    [Parameter(Mandatory=$True,Position=2)]
    [int]$StorageSrvPort
)


$connection = New-Object System.Net.Sockets.
TcpClient($StorageSrvAdd, $StorageSrvPort)
if ($connection.Connected) {
    Return "Port "+$StorageSrvPort+" is accessable on the
"+$StorageSrvAdd
}
else {
    Return "Port "+$StorageSrvPort+" is inaccessable on the
"+$StorageSrvAdd
}
```

vSphere hosts have built-in firewalls, though when you enable the iSCSI initiator, exceptions are automatically added by the vSphere hosts. To enable rules for iSCSI manually, you can either use command line utilities or the vSphere client. For this perform the following steps:

1. Open **Security Profile** of a vSphere host.
2. Open the **Properties** of the firewall.
3. Scroll down to **Software iSCSI Client**. Check the **Software iSCSI Client** to enable it.
4. If you want to get it accessed from certain IP Addresses, click on the **Firewall** button below.
5. Select **Only allow connections from the following network**.

6. Enter a subnet or subnets as shown in the following screenshot:

7. Use esxcli network firewall to set up the firewall rules manually.

8. Make sure you have network connectivity to the iSCSI storage array. The easiest way to check it is by using the `ping` command from your vSphere host:

```
ping storage001.linxsol.com
```

or

```
vmkping storage001.linxsol.com
```

9. If you have enabled jumbo frames (in my case, I have enabled them) make sure their configuration is correct on both the vSphere host and on the storage device end. You can use the `vmkping` command to verify this:

```
vmkping -s 9000 storage001.linxsol.com -d
```

10. Always perform a storage device rescan whenever you add, remove, or change the configuration. The rescan process is logged in `/var/log/` messages. You can perform a rescan as follows:

```
vi-admin@vma:~[crimv3esx001.linxsol.com]> esxcli storage core adapter rescan --adapter vmhba0
```

11. Then you can scan for the datastores:

```
vmkfstools -V
```

If you are using CHAP authentication for your vSphere host iSCSI initiator, you should be able to troubleshoot it. For example, if CHAP secret is incorrect, your vSphere host will be able to scan the LUNs to be mounted but will have an access problem. You can start looking into `/var/log/syslog.log` for CHAP errors.

Follow these steps to verify the CHAP settings:

1. Go to the vSphere host **Configuration** tab and click on **Storage Adapters**.

2. Choose **Software iSCSI Adapter** and go to its **Properties**.

3. Select **CHAP** from the **General** tab and verify your secret.

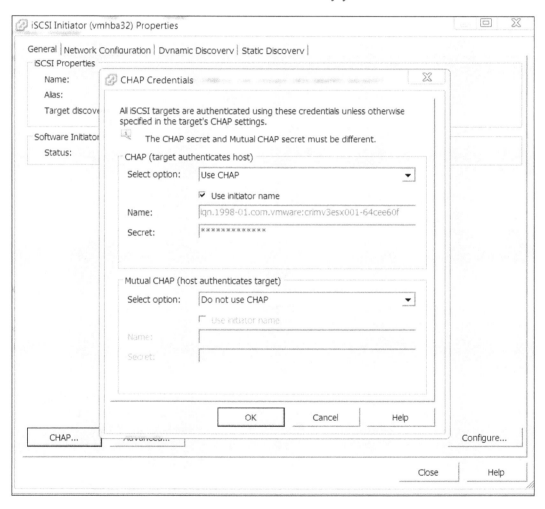

iSCSI error correction

iSCSI protocol is shipped with error correction methods called header digests and data digests. These digests verify the data integrity traveling on any side between iSCSI initiators and iSCSI targets. They are also able to verify the network routes, switches, and the complete communication path.

These digests are not enabled by default, so you need to enable them. Follow these steps to enable the header digests and the data digests:

1. Go to the vSphere host's **Configuration** tab and click on **Storage Adapters**.
2. Choose **Software iSCSI Adapter** and go to its **Properties**.
3. Select **Advanced** from the **General** tab.
4. From the **Advanced Settings**, change the **Header Digest** to **Required**.
5. Then repeat the preceding steps for **Data Digest** and click **OK**.

Troubleshooting NFS issues

NFS issues are very much similar to iSCSI issues. Some of the common problems and how these can be resolved effectively have been discussed here.

If you are having an error of denying mount request by an NFS server, make sure the NFS server has published the exports and appropriate permissions are set up for the client to access the exports.

In your NFS server, make sure the `no_root_squash` option exists in `/etc/exports`; alternatively, follow your NAS manual to set it up. If it is not set up, you will get an access error. It will get more complicated when you will be able to create a datastore but unable to create a virtual machine. In some NAS, `anon=0` is used in `/etc/exports` instead of using `no_root_squash`.

Always make sure the portmap and NFS services are running if you are facing mount fail problem.

Verify the firewall settings: the NFS client requires access to TCP ports 111, 896, and 2049 to be opened on your NFS server. You can troubleshoot it using the script provided in the section on *Troubleshooting iSCSI-related issues* in this chapter. Timeouts, slow connectivity, or mount failure could also be the cause of firewall. Similar symptoms can be seen in cases of providing a bad DNS.

Use TCP rather than UDP with vSphere hosts to access NFS exports. If you are unable to mount a volume, you can try to identify the problem by looking into `/var/log/vmkernel` or in `/proc/vmware/log`.

VMware best practice advises that NIC teaming failback should be set to `no` as this will avoid any unexpected behavior if something bad happens with your network. Use the following timeout values in your vSphere host **Advanced Settings** tab as recommended by VMware:

`NFS.HeartbeatTimeout = 5`

`NFS.HeartbeatFrequency = 12`

`NFS.HeartbeatMaxFailures = 10`

Troubleshooting VMFS issues

VMFS is a high performance distributed filesystem. VMFS version 5 supports up to 60 TB of file size. Here are some important guidelines you should consider when working with VMFS volumes:

- If you are not able to store files from 2 TB to 60 TB, make sure the partition table is using GPT instead of MBR. You can use `partedUtil` to view the partitioning.
- The free space threshold value of a VMFS as suggested by VMware is 200 MB, and once 100 MB space is left, you will start having problems.
- Always watch carefully how your space grows on a VMFS volume; if you have a less space, it will likely cause slow performance in issuing commands such as `ls`, `copy`, and so on.
- Don't leave snapshots too long, and keep reclaiming the space by committing or removing the snapshots whenever it is possible. Snapshots keep growing and slow down the performance as well.

You can always use the `vmkfstools` command to manage and view the information about the VMFS volume, as seen in the following screenshot:

```
10.2.6.93 - PuTTY
vi-admin@vma:~[crimv3esx001.linxsol.com ]> vmkfstools

Synopsis: /usr/bin/vmkfstools OPTIONS [<diskpath>]

Command-specific options:
   --adapterType
     -a

         The adapter type of a disk to be created. Accepts buslogic, lsilogic
         or ide.

   --blocksize
     -b

         The block size of the VMFS file system to create. When omitted, the
         creation defaults to using 1MB for the blocksize.

   --clonevirtualdisk
     -i

         Create a copy of a virtual disk or raw disk. The copy will be in
         the specified disk format. Takes source disk as argument.

   --createfs
     -C

         Creates a VMFS file system, requires -S, and optionally -b

   --createrdm
     -r

         Creates raw disk mapping, takes the disk device path.
         Map a raw disk to a file on a VMFS file system. Once the mapping
         is established, it can be used to access the raw disk like a
         normal VMFS virtual disk. The 'file length' of the mapping is
         the same as the size of the raw disk that it points to.

   --createrdmpassthru
     -z
```

VMFS snapshots and resignaturing

You have already learned that each LUN in VMFS is assigned a UUID. This UUID is produced by VMware and contains a hexadecimal number that is stored in the superblock of the filesystem. The unique LUN ID of the original LUN is also stored in the VMFS metadata. When you perform a replication operation on a LUN, the replicated LUN is completely identical to the source LUN; even the UUID of the LUN remains the same. For this particular reason, before you mount the newly created LUN, you need to resignature it. The vSphere host can identify if a LUN is an identical LUN and holds a VMFS copy and thus not mount it. You should consider the following points before proceeding:

- There is no comeback once you resignature the datastore
- The newly copied LUN will be treated as a new datastore
- A datastore cannot be resignatured if all its extents are not online

Perform the following steps for reassigning a new signature:

1. Use your vSphere client and go to **Configuration** and then to **Storage**.
2. Click on **Add Storage**, following which the wizard will appear.
3. From the **Storage Type**, select **Disk/LUN** and click **Next**.
4. Select the storage device you would like to add and click **Next**.
5. From **Select VMFS Mount Options**, choose the second option: **Assign a new signature**.
6. Click **Next** and then **Finish**.

SAN display problems

When your vSphere host does not display SANs correctly, you are required to use different troubleshooting techniques to make it work correctly.

It may happen that you are not able to find a port. This could be because of a disconnected network cable. Ensure that your cables are connected correctly; your link is up if you are able to find a green color link light else, replace the cable.

If your routes are not published correctly, you will have connectivity issues among different subnets of your LAN segments. Ensure your storage segment is accessible to the vSphere host's segments and correct routes are published between the subnets. Verify your settings of gateway address, IP address and subnet mask on SAN as well as in your vSphere hosts.

As mentioned previously, for iSCSI-based SANs, make sure the CHAP settings and the secret are correct. For iSCSI and NFS, make sure the access list allows your vSphere hosts to access the storage. For iSCSI and NFS clients' access, also make sure the access of the subnet is configured correctly in the firewall properties of the vSphere host.

Whenever you create, modify, and delete LUNs, perform a rescan. Also perform a rescan when you reconnect a disconnected cable, if you have modified host settings, or if the discovery address or CHAP settings have been changed.

For a SAN with multiple storage processors, ensure active processors are correctly configured, and publish the LUNs accessible by vSphere hosts.

Ensure your VMkernel network port of vSphere hosts can access iSCSI storage.

SAN performance troubleshooting

Sometimes, slow SAN performance kills your infrastructure. It can be caused due to multiple issues. This may also require you to sometimes reproduce the problem to identify the issues and to troubleshoot it. Use `esxtop` to troubleshoot and monitor storage performance from the vSphere host as seen in the earlier chapter. Remove volume caching in order to get the real statistics. Analyze the performance of various I/O sets. You can use free open source tools to measure I/O loads. Use IOMeter available at `http://goo.gl/RnDFyS` to simulate I/O loads.

Use `esxtop` while IOMeter is running from a virtual machine and capture the storage performance, for example:

```
esxtop -a -b 7 -n 700 > performance_data.out
```

Ensure your multi-path settings are working correctly. Use advanced techniques like Disk Alignment to ensure the data drives are aligned correctly for efficient high I/O. From your SAN, use the built-in tools, if provided, to check the SAN performance as well.

Summary

The chapter covered different storage troubleshooting techniques except fiber SANs. Learning these techniques is a good starting point to manage most storage troubleshooting issues. The focus is also on VMware vMA appliances to deploy troubleshooting procedures for storage. You have learned how to troubleshoot storage architecture, multipathing, and PSA issues. You have also learned how to use and modify claim rules for storage LUNs. Later in the chapter, I covered iSCSI troubleshooting and how the iSCSI sense codes are used by storage devices to inform about path down states. NFS and VMFS datastore troubleshooting was also covered step by step using different techniques. We will discuss troubleshooting vSphere host issues and vSphere high availability agent in the next chapters.

6
Advanced Troubleshooting of vCenter Server and vSphere Hosts

This last chapter presents a quick walkthrough of some of the common vCenter Server issues. Here, I have covered some of the issues using a vCenter Server 6.0 application. The vCenter statistics that were introduced in the *Chapter 1*, *The Methodology of Problem Solving*, have been discussed in detail. The appliance is based on SUSE Linux and is available to download from VMware's website. In the latest VMware vCenter, the way SSL certificates are deployed has changed. It is much easier for system engineers to replace and manage the certificates of vCenter Server and vSphere hosts. This chapter also covers the vSphere HA agent troubleshooting, disabling and re-enabling it, and completely reinstalling it. Finally, we will look into vSphere network isolation problems and auto-deployment problems of vCenter Server. The following topics are covered in this chapter:

- vCenter Server managed hosts
- vCenter Server SSL certificates
- Regenerating certificates
- vCenter Server database
- vSphere HA agent troubleshooting
- Unreachable or uninitialized state
- HA agent initialization error
- HA agent host failed state
- Network partitioned or network isolated errors
- Commonly known auto deploy problems

vCenter managed hosts

VMware vCenter Server is a centralized management platform that provides extendibility and control of VMware vSphere hosts from a central console. In order to get full functionality, you must use vCenter Server for your vSphere hosts. It will simplify your overall management of the multiple vSphere hosts. In the following table, you can see the VMware vCenter Server management capabilities:

A single vCenter can support up to:	
vSphere hosts	1,000
Powered on VMs	10,000
Hosts per cluster	64
VMs per cluster	6,000
In Linked Mode, you can have up to:	
vCenter server	10
Powered on VMs	30,000
Hosts per cluster	64
VMs per cluster	8,000

Logging for an inventory service

Logging for an inventory service needs to be configured for a better troubleshooting experience. For this purpose, the logging level of vCenter Server Inventory Service should be set to **Trace**. Sometimes, when you use the vSphere web client, you cannot see the inventory tree loading in the client, or the client is not able to log in to the vCenter Server. Sometimes you could also find that the properties or objects in the web client are not updated or are missing. Log levels can be reduced or increased based on your requirements. There are different logging verbosity levels available, from **Trace, Debug, Info, Warn** to **Error**. Follow these steps to configure the logging level for vCenter Server Inventory Service:

1. For a Windows-based vCenter Server, log in as an administrator and open **Services**.

2. From the list, select **vCenter Server Inventory Service** and right-click on it.

3. Select **Stop** from the menu to stop the service. For a vCenter Server appliance, type the following command:

   ```
   service vmware-inventoryservice stop
   ```

4. Browse to the following directory location for Windows-based vCenter Server:

   ```
   %PROGRAMFILES%\VMware\Infrastructure\Inventory Service\lib\server\
   config
   ```

5. For vCenter Server appliance:

   ```
   /usr/lib/vmware-vpx/inventoryservice/lib/server/config
   ```

6. Use Notepad in Windows vCenter or vi in the vCenter appliance to open the `log4j.properties` file and edit the following lines as shown in this table:

Old value	New value
log4j.logger.com.vmware.vim=INFO	log4j.logger.com.vmware.vim=TRACE
log4j.appender.LOGFILE. Threshold=INFO	log4j.appender.LOGFILE. Threshold=TRACE

7. Start the vCenter Server Inventory Service in Windows-based vCenter Server from the service console and for the vCenter Server application, using the following command:

   ```
   service vmware-inventoryservicestart
   ```

Viewing vCenter Server logs

Let's quickly walk through how to use the log browser:

1. Log in to your vSphere web client using administrator credentials.

2. On the left pane, click on **Log Browser**, and in the **View** pane on your right, click on **Select Object**. This will open up a new window from where you can select vCenter Server in your environment.

3. Once the vCenter Server is selected, you can choose the log file you would like to view from the **Type** dropdown menu.

4. From here, you can browse different log files from different objects.

5. You can also click on **Refresh** for the latest logs.

Setting up vCenter Server the statistics intervals from vSphere Web Client

We discussed setting up statistics intervals in the *Chapter 2, Monitoring and Troubleshooting Host and VM Performance*. We will see how to configure statistics intervals from the vSphere web client. By default, vCenter Server collects statistics of its vSphere environment periodically and stores them. You can not only tweak these settings but also control how to display the gathered information. Tweaking this can help you to perform better troubleshooting and generate performance reports to identify any performance issues. You can enable or disable the default statistical data collection. You can select the different time intervals to collect the statistical data, how long that data should be saved, and to what level the statistical information should be collected.

vSphere hosts collect the statistics for all the metrics every 20 seconds and store the collected data through the performance manager locally for an hour. vCenter Server collects this data using its performance manager from the remote vSphere hosts at specified time intervals. Once the data is collected, vCenter Server stores it in its database. The metrics can be displayed later on using the vSphere client:

1. Log in to your vSphere web client.

2. Select the vCenter Server from the **Inventory** Lists and click on the server name you want to configure.

3. Click on the **Manage** tab and then click on **General**.

4. Click on the **Edit** button. This will open the vCenter Server settings.

5. In the **Statistics** window, you can configure the **Statistics** level, the interval duration to capture them, the time to save them, and disable and enable them.

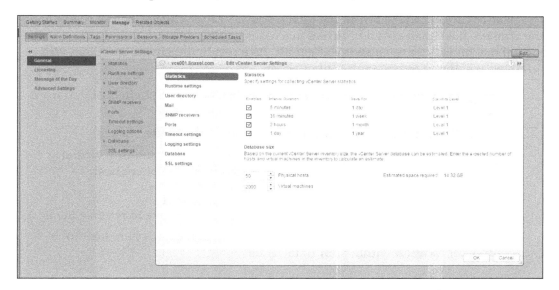

The following table briefly describes the statistics log levels:

Statistics Level	Description
Level 1	Collects statistics of CPU, memory, disk, network, system, virtual machine operations and cluster services. This level is selected by default.
Level 2	In addition to Level 1, collects statistics of all disk, memory, and virtual machine operations metrics. It is used when you need to monitor more than basic statistics and you want to implement monitoring for longer periods. It doesn't include device statistics.
Level 3	It includes everything from Level 1 and Level 2, along with collected device statistics. This includes CPU usage of a vSphere host for a single CPU or statistics of a single virtual machine. You can enable it to troubleshoot a problem and then disable it once the problem is diagnosed.
Level 4	All metrics are collected. It is not recommended to enable it for longer periods, as the data will be collected in large amounts. You can use it just like Level 3 for short periods of times.

Relocating or removing a vSphere host

A cluster is formed with multiple vSphere hosts. When we remove a vSphere host, its resources are subtracted from the total resources of the cluster. Before removing the vSphere host, migrate your virtual machines to other hosts. If you don't need the virtual machines, you must switch them off. As a result, the virtual machines will be removed when you remove the vSphere host.

1. Log in to your vCenter Server and right-click on the vSphere host you want to remove.

2. From the pop-up menu, select **Enter Maintenance Mode**.

3. You may need to wait for some time for the transfer of running virtual machines from the selected vSphere host to another vSphere host.

4. Click **Yes** to confirm the transfer.

5. Right-click on the vSphere host again and select **Remove** to remove the host.

6. You can also repeat these steps if you want to move a vSphere host to another location within your data center.

vSphere host disconnection and reconnection

Sometimes, you need to disconnect a vSphere host from the vCenter Server console. When you disconnect a vSphere host, vCenter Server stops monitoring the vSphere host temporarily, but it doesn't remove it from the vCenter Server. You can still see the vSphere host in the disconnected state along with its associated virtual machines in the inventory. Instead, when you remove a vSphere host from vCenter Server, the vSphere host and the virtual machines related to it are removed. You can disconnect a host from the vSphere client with the following steps:

1. Log in to your vSphere client.

2. Select the vSphere host you want to disconnect and right-click on it.

3. From the menu, select **Disconnect**, and click **Yes** to confirm.

4. The host will be disconnected. See the following screenshot of a disconnected host:

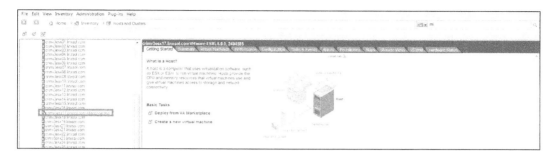

5. You can reconnect the vSphere host again by right-clicking and selecting the **Connect** option from the menu.

vSphere SSL certificates

In vSphere 6.0, you can implement and replace the SSL certificates in a much easier way compared to older versions. VMware has modified the vSphere SSL architecture to simplify the overall SSL certificate management process. Different vSphere components use SSL certificates to authenticate with each other and use an **Security Assertion Markup Language** (**SAML**) token for authentication. SAML is described as an XML standard that allows secured web domains to the exchange user information, for example, user authentication and authorization data. A reverse HTTP proxy is used to provide certificate information to different vSphere services. vSphere 6.0 has introduced the **VMware Certificate Authority** (**VMCA**) to deploy SSL certificates to vSphere hosts, vCenter Server, vCenter Single Sign-on service, and other services. The vSphere Certificate Manager, which is a command line utility, can be used to replace or add the certificates. You can also replace the certificates manually.

Now, VMware VMCA does most of the certificate management. vSphere hosts and vCenter Server and its services use VMCA as their root **certificate authority** (**CA**), and self-signed certificates are replaced by the certificates signed by VMCA. You can use any one of the two processes to deploy your SSL certificates using VMCA.

You can replace the VMCA root certificate with your own CA signed certificate, for example, with a GoDaddy root certificate. VMCA will deploy the certificates to your vSphere infrastructure.

If you cannot use intermediate certificates, you can replace the certificates manually. For this purpose, you can also use vSphere Certificate Manager utility if you do not want to replace certificates manually. **VMware Directory Services (VMDird)**, manages SAML token for authentication with vCenter SSO services. **VMware Authentication Framework Daemon (VMAFD)** consists of **VMware Endpoint Certificate Store (VECS)** and numerous other authentication services. VECS is used as a local (client-server) key store to store different kind of SSL certificates, private keys, and all the trust information regarding these certificates.

vSphere Certificates	Managed by	Store Name
vSphere Host Certificates	VMCA	`/etc/vmware/ssl`
Machine SSL Certificate (MACHINE_SSL_CERT)	VMCA	VECS
Solution User Certificates (machine, vpxd, vpxd-extensions, vSphere-web client)	VMCA	VECS
vCenter SSO Service Certificate	vCenter Installer	Only use vSphere client to replace it but stored on the local disk.

All of the preceding components including VMCA are part of embedded Platform Service Controller deployment of a vCenter Server. VMCA is shipped with `certool.exe` located in `C:\Program Files\VMware\vCenter Server\vmcad` or in vCenter appliance `/usr/lib/vmware-vmca/bin/certool`, while VECS can be managed by `vecs-cli`. The vSphere Certificate Manager utility that we will use now to perform management of SSL certificates is located in `C:\Program Files\VMware\vCenter Server\vmcad\certificate-manager.bat` in Windows. In Linux, it is located in `/usr/lib/vmware-vmca/bin/certificate-manager`.

Replacing machine certificates

The HTTP reverse proxy service uses an SSL certificate on **Platform Services Controllers (PSC)** on all the management nodes and in embedded deployment. You need to provide the following information when replacing SSL certificates using vSphere Certificate Manager:

- Administrator password of vSphere
- Custom certificate authority file
- Custom SSL certificate file
- Custom SSL key file

A certificate must be in CRT format and x509 version 3. Its key size should be 2048 bits or more and it should be encoded in PEM format. The certificate's `SubjectAltName` should consist of DNS Name = `Machine.FQDN`. Further, it should also contain key usages digital signature, key encipherment, and non-repudiation:

1. Go to the `/usr/lib/vmware-vmca/bin` directory and run Certificate-Manager:

   ```
   ./certificate-manager
   ```

2. Select the first option: **Replace Machine SSL certificate with Custom Certificate**.

3. The certificate-manager utility will ask for your vCenter Server SSO password. Enter the password when prompted.

4. After entering the correct password, certificate-manager utility will display two options. Choose the second option: **Import custom certificate(s) and key(s)** to replace existing Machine SSL certificate.

5. In the next step, type the custom certificate path.

6. Repeat the preceding step for the key file

7. Repeat the preceding step for the root certificate.

8. If you are replacing custom certificates for the first time, you will be prompted to provide the information into the `certool.cfg` file:

   ```
   Please configure certool.cfg file with proper values before
   proceeding to next step.
   Press Enter key to skip optional parameters or use Default value.
   Enter proper value for 'Country' [Default value : US] :Italy
   Enter proper value for 'Name' [Default value : Acme] :LinxSol
   Enter proper value for 'Organization' [Default value : AcmeOrg]
   :Linx ICT Solutions
   Enter proper value for 'OrgUnit' [Default value : AcmeOrg
   Engineering] :Information Technology
   Enter proper value for 'State' [Default value : California] :Milan
   Enter proper value for 'Locality' [Default value : Palo Alto]
   :Viale Monte Nero
   Enter proper value for 'IPAddress' [optional] :
   Enter proper value for 'Email' [Default value : email@acme.com]
   :zeeshan@linxsol.com
   Enter proper value for 'Hostname' [Enter valid Fully Qualified
   Domain Name(FQDN), For Example : example.domain.com] :vcenter001.
   linxsol.com
   ```

9. Type yes (Y) to confirm.

10. If everything goes well, it will display the `Status: 100% Completed [All tasks completed successfully]` message on the CLI.

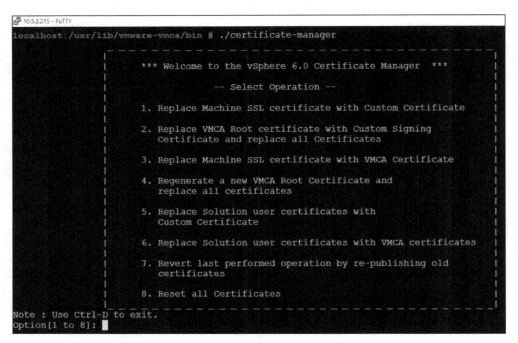

Replacing VMCA root certificate

In the certificate chain, a VMCA self-signed certificate can be replaced with a CA-signed certificate, which includes VMCA as an intermediate certificate. We will use vSphere Certificate Manager to replace the root certificate with a CA-signed certificate by performing the following steps:

1. Run the certificate-manager tool:

   `./certificate-manager`

2. Select the second choice from the wizard: **Replace VMCA Root certificate with Custom Signing Certificate and replace all Certificates**.

3. When prompted, enter your vCenter Server SSO password.

4. Next, select the first option: **Generate Certificate Signing Request(s) and Key(s)** for VMCA Root Signing certificate.

5. Enter the path where certificate-manager can generate your **Certificate Signing Request** (CSR) and key.

6. Sign your CSR using your CA.

Replacing user solution certificates

You can replace the existing solution user certificates with a CA-signed certificate using certificate-manager, as follows:

1. Run the certificate-manager tool:

   `./certificate-manager`

2. Select the fifth option from the wizard: **Replace Solution user certificates with Custom Certificates**.

3. When prompted, enter your vCenter Server SSO password.

4. Select the second option and provide the custom CA-signed certificate file location.

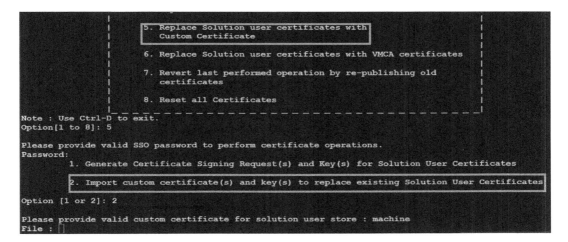

With the help of the certificate-manager, you can revert your last deployed certificates and go one step back in time. Run the certificate-manager, choose option 7, and follow the prompts by answering.

Implementing SSL certificates for ESXi

In vSphere 6.0, when you add a vSphere host into the vCenter Server, VMCA assigns a new certificate to the host automatically. If you replace the VMCA-issued certificate with a CA-signed certificate later on as described in previous exercises, you also need to replace the certificates in vSphere hosts. This can be easily done through the vSphere web client:

1. Log in to your vSphere web client.

2. Click on the vCenter Server and choose the vSphere host you want to renew the certificate.

3. Right-click on the vSphere host and from the menu and select **Certificates**.

4. Then click on **Renew Certificates**.

5. When prompted by the confirmation dialog box of **Renew Certificate**, select **Yes**.

6. Refresh your browser. You will see that the certificate has been re-issued.

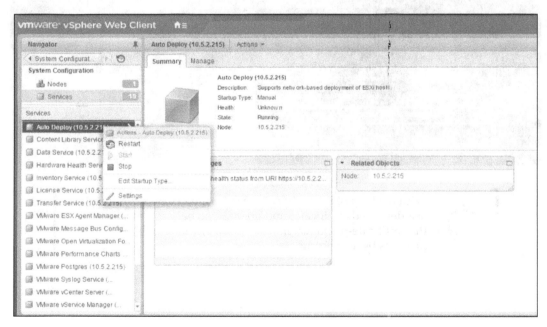

Regenerating certificates

The VMCA root certificate can be regenerated and machine SSL certificates can be replaced with a VMCA-signed certificate. You can also replace the solution user certificates with regenerated certificates.

1. Run the certificate-manager tool.

   `./certificate-manager`

2. Select the fourth option from the wizard: `Regenerate a new VMCA Root Certificate and replace all certificates.`

3. When prompted, enter your vCenter Server SSO administrator password.

4. Click **Yes** when prompted to continue the operation.

5. All the services will be restarted at this point, and you will be able to see the status progress of regenerating the certificates on the CLI prompt.

6. Once successfully completed, the **All tasks completed successfully** message will be displayed on the screen.

> If you are having troubles with the vSpehre client in your web browser, make sure to delete old certificates from the browser.

vCenter Server database

On Windows-based vCenter Server, installation fails if the Microsoft SQL Server database is using compatibility mode because of an unsupported version. Before installation of vCenter Server, you should ensure that the MSSQL version you are going to use is supported by VMware vCenter Server.

> This error also can occur even if you are using a supported MSSQL version, but it is configuring to run in compatibility mode. It will raise the following error message:
>
> The DB user entered does not have the required permissions needed to install and configure vCenter Server with the selected DB. Please correct the following error(s): %s. The error can be solved by using the supported database for vCenter.

vSphere HA agent troubleshooting

vSphere HA host states are reported by vCenter Server when there are some errors in your vSphere hosts. When working with vSphere infrastructure in a highly available environment, you may encounter different kinds of errors that prevent vSphere HA from working correctly, for example, HA agent on `crimvlesx002.linxsol.com` in cluster Cluster-ML-FT in DataCenter017-Milan has an error or insufficient resources to satisfy HA failover level on cluster. This is followed by agent error, vSphere HA agent cannot be correctly installed or configured, Internal AAM Errors - agent couldn't start, and so on.

In this topic, we will discuss possible causes and troubleshooting tips to solve these issues. A good starting point for troubleshooting HA agents' errors could be VMkernel logs that you can find in `/var/log`, as discussed in previous chapters.

As the VMware Knowledge Base suggests (`http://kb.vmware.com/selfservice/microsites/search.do?language=en_US&cmd=displayKC&externalId=2007739`), check if your vSphere host is in the lockdown mode. You can use power shell to verify this using the following command:

```
Get-vmhost crimvlesx001.linxsol.com | select Name, @{N="LockDown";E={$_.
Extensiondata.Config.adminDisabled}} | ft -auto Name, LockDown
```

If your vSphere host is in `Lockdown` mode, you can use the following command to exit from the mode:

```
(Get-vmhost crimvlesx001.linxsol.com | get-view).ExitLockdownMode()
```

You can also verify it from the vSphere web client:

1. Select your vSphere host and go to **Manage**.
2. Go to **Settings** and then to **Security Profile**.
3. Scroll down to **Lockdown Mode**.
4. You can verify if your vSphere host is in **Disabled**, **Normal**, or **Strict** mode.

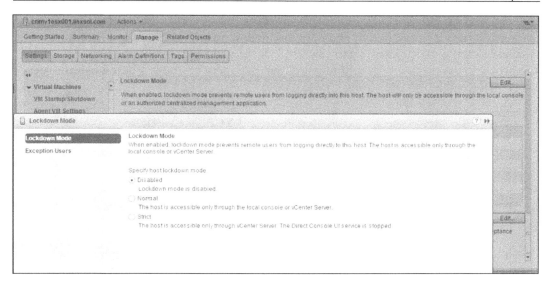

Unreachable or uninitialized state

The vSphere HA agent becomes uninitialized on a vSphere host. When a master vSphere host or vCenter Server tries to contact to the agent of the vSphere host and it doesn't respond, it is declared to be in the uninitialized state. There could be multiple possible reasons why a vSphere host is uninitialized. When an HA agent gets uninitialized, the vSphere host is not able to reach any datastores, not even the local datastore where the vSphere host HA caches the state information of HA agent.

You should also check the firewall ports on your vSphere hosts if they are open for the vSphere HA agent to communicate with other hosts and the vCenter Server. The vSphere HA Agent uses port 8182 for communication. You can check the event log from the vSphere client to find out the reason.

It is logged as vSphere HA Agent for the host that has an error. You should make sure the datastores are accessible by the vSphere host. For troubleshooting datastores, you can follow the guidelines given in *Chapter 5, Monitoring and Troubleshooting Storage*. If the problem persists, you should reinstall the HA agent on the vSphere host (the topic will be covered in the upcoming context).

Incoming Ports	Outgoing Ports	TCP	UDP
8042		✓	✓
8045		✓	✓
8182	8182	✓	✓
	2050	✓	✓
	2250	✓	✓

A vSphere HA agent is declared in an unreachable state when a vSphere master host is unable to contact a secondary vSphere host. In this scenario, the vSphere HA stops monitoring the virtual machines and is unable to maintain them. It might be as simple as a networking problem, where vCenter Server is unable to reach the vSphere HA agent, or as complicated where all vSphere hosts in a given cluster have failed. vCenter Server cannot communicate to the HA agent when you disable the vSphere HA agent on hosts and then re-enable it. If a vSphere HA agent fails, the watchdog process tries to restart it, but if the watchdog service fails to restart the HA agent, the HA agent is declared to be unreachable. You can follow the guidelines given in *Chapter 4, Monitoring and Troubleshooting Networking*. You should also make sure your cluster is not having any failures. If it still doesn't resolve the HA agent problem, you should reinstall the vSphere HA agent on your vSphere hosts by following the topic *Reinstalling HA agent* discussed later in this chapter:

The HA agent initialization error

The HA agent can also produce the operation timed out error. Removing a vSphere host and adding it again to the cluster doesn't solve the problem. Here is how you can resolve it:

1. Log in to your vSphere client.
2. Disable **High Availability** on the cluster.
3. Select a vSphere host and go to the **Configuration** tab.
4. Click on **Security Profile** in the left column.
5. Click on **Properties** and verify the status of vSphere **High Availability**.
6. Set the service to start and stop automatically, and start if it the service is stopped.
7. Enable HA again on the cluster and reconfigure it.

Reinstalling the HA agent

If you want to reinstall the `vpxa` agent into your vSphere hosts without losing their database entries, you can perform the following procedure without affecting the running virtual machines. To reconfigure the HA agent from the vSphere client, follow these steps:

1. Log in to your vSphere client.

2. Select a vSphere Host in a cluster where you want to perform reconfiguration.

3. Right-click on the vSphere host and choose the last option: **Reconfigure vSphere for HA**.

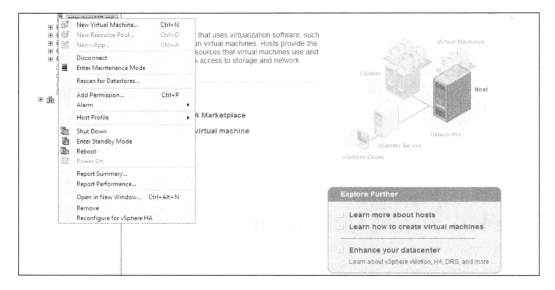

To reinstall the HA agent manually, follow this process:

1. Right-click on the vSphere host and click on **Disconnect** to disconnect it from the vCenter Server.

2. Now log in to your vSphere host using SSH.

3. Delete vpxuser by logging in to the vSphere client and **Local Users & Groups** and then **Users**.

4. Remove the vpxuser user.

5. Remove the vpxa agent from your vSphere host:

   ```
   chmod +x /opt/vmware/uninstallers/VMware-fdm-uninstall.sh
   cd /opt/vmware/uninstallers/
   ./VMware-fdm-uninstall.sh
   ```

6. Reconnect your vSphere host in vCenter Server. The vpxauser will be created again automatically.

```
~ # cd /opt/vmware/uninstallers/
/opt/vmware/uninstallers # ls
VMware-fdm-uninstall.sh
/opt/vmware/uninstallers #  ./VMware-fdm-uninstall.sh
```

HA agent host failed state

A vSphere master is considered to be in a failed state when it is unable to communicate with vCenter Server. This condition is not always reported correctly by vCenter Server, and at times, it can be generated falsely. The actual condition can be caused by a vSphere HA master when it is not able to reach to its heartbeat datastores. It is resolved automatically if a vSphere host is in a temporary failed state.

The possible cause could be a failure in accessing the heartbeat datastores. The heartbeat datastores' reachability can also be caused by network errors. You can apply the network and storage troubleshooting skills you have learned in previous chapters to resolve vSphere host in a failed state.

Network partitioned or network isolated errors

It may so happen that your vSphere host is randomly or permanently turning into red and you are getting one of the following messages in your alarm list: vSphere HA detected a network-partitioned host; Status = Red or vSphere HA detected that host crimv1esx001.linxsol.com is in a different network partition than the master Cluster-ML-FL in DataCenter017-Milan.

As suggested by VMware, this type of problem can be caused when your vCenter Server is able to communicate with the vSphere hosts by using heartbeat datastores but the communication between vCenter Server and vSphere hosts is disconnected on the management network. In this condition, a vSphere host is not considered as an isolated host.

While a vSphere host is considered to be in a network isolated state when it is unable to ping the configured isolation addresses and the vSphere HA agents on the other cluster hosts are unable to communicate with its vSphere host HA agent. VMware HA then issues this type of error: `Could not reach isolation address: 10.2.6.12`.

Isolation addresses are configured on vSphere HA cluster to confirm the cluster functionally by sending and receiving response from the addresses. By default, the isolation address is the default gateway of your network, but you can configure the different network address for different clusters according to your requirements. You can see the following screenshot:

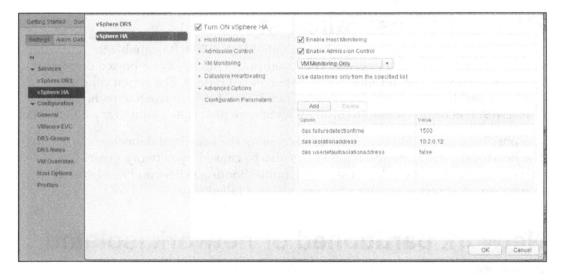

The possible causes for this problem could be:

- Mismatched VLAN information
- Network configuration
- NIC's speed mode (auto negotiate, 100, 1000 half duplex/full duplex)
- NIC teaming (policy exceptions)
- Misconfigured switch
- Mismatched IPv4/IPv6

The problem can be resolved by verifying the preceding configuration. For this purpose, you can use the different tools and procedures mentioned in *Chapter 4, Monitoring and Troubleshooting Networking*.

Commonly known auto deploy problems

Let's understand the auto deploy procedure in vCenter Server 6. The vCenter Server 6.0 is being adopted by the industry rapidly. Here's a quick walkthrough of the new auto deployment procedure in vCenter Server appliance and troubleshooting its known issues:

1. Log in to your vSphere web client.
2. From the left panel, select **Administration** and click.
3. In the **Administration** panel, expand the **Deployment** tab.
4. Select **System Configuration** and choose **Services**.
5. Under **Services**, select the first service: **Auto Deploy**.
6. From the **Action** menu, you can **Start**, **Stop**, or **Restart** the auto deploy service.
7. You can also choose between the option to start the auto deploy service with the vCenter Server automatically or manually.

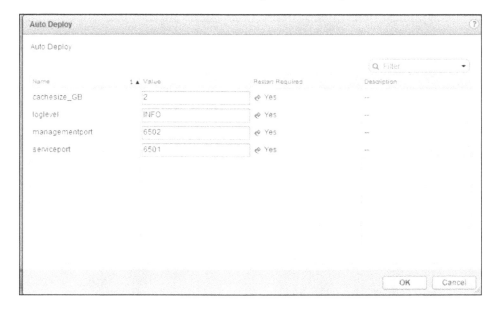

8. To change the **Management** port of the auto deploy service, click on the **Manage** tab and then click on the **Edit** button. By default, the management port is listening on 6502 and the service port is listening on 6501.

9. You can also change the log level and cache size from the **Manage** tab.

10. To download the auto deploy logs, click on the vCenter Server and select **Auto Deploy**.

11. You can click on **Download Auto Deploy** log files. You can also verify the **iPXE Boot URL** from the **Configuration** area of **Auto Deploy** window.

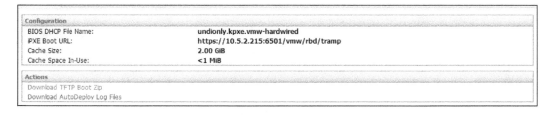

12. Next, you need to configure the DHCP server. You can create a new DHCP scope in your infrastructure, and in the **scope** options, configure Boot Server Host Name and Bootfile Name. You should configure the TFTP server address in the Boot Server Host Name and in the Bootfile `undionly.kpxe.vmw-hardwired`, which is your BIOS DHCP File Name and can be found in the Auto Deploy configuration (see the preceding screenshot).

13. The DHCP scope options can vary from vendor to vendor. You may find them to be different in Windows operating systems and in Dell SonicWALL Firewalls.

14. Configure the TFTP server of your choice and download the TFTP Boot Zip from your **Auto Deploy** configuration window to place it into your TFTP server.

15. Other issues also occur if there is a firewall involved. Make sure your TFTP connections are allowed in the aftpd daemon in vCenter Server. The auto deploy ports are open and accessible. You can use iptables not only for troubleshooting TFTP but you can also view the accessible and blocked services by the firewall on a vCenter Server appliance.

16. Though this is out of scope of this book, here's a quick `iptable` command to allow port 69:

```
iptables -A port_filter -m state --state NEW -i eth0 -p udp --dport
69 -j ACCEPT
```

17. As you can see in the preceding screenshot, IPtables ruleset for vCenter Server is added into the `port_filter` chain, which also makes it easier to understand and troubleshoot.

18. Similarly, if a host is not booting from the correct ESXi image profile, you can use the `Test-DeployRuleSetCompliance` and `Repair-DeployeRuleSetCompliance` cmdlets can be used to correct the rule set from the PowerCLI. To verify the rule set compliance for all hosts, run the following command:

```
Get-VMHost | Test-DeployRuleSetCompliance
```

19. You can repair it as follows:

```
Get-VMHost | Test-DeployRuleSetCompliance | Repair-
DeployRuleSetCompliance
```

Getting help

VMware Community found at https://communities.vmware.com/welcome, is the best forum to get free advice about different problems of VMware vSphere hosts and vCenter Server. You can search and find the solutions of existing problems as well as discuss the new problems in order to find their solutions. A subpart of VMware Community is VMware Technology Network, which has excellent and in-depth technical resources for developers to system engineers. You can discuss peer to peer, post in forums, and get advice from the best virtualization gurus in the industry.

To remain up to date with technical skills, you can join **VMware User Group (VMUG)** at https://www.vmug.com.

Summary

In this chapter, you saw different vCenter Server and vSphere HA agent and state problems. You also learned how to troubleshoot and fix some of the common problems. Once you know how to fix some of the common issues, you get some background of troubleshooting for advanced problems as well. You can then simply follow the work flow of problems and troubleshoot step by step.

This concludes the last chapter of this book, which provided some fundamental steps to troubleshoot vSphere based infrastructures.

A
Learning PowerGUI Basics

PowerGUI is a cool tool used to speed up the PowerShell implementation. You can use it to manage not only your vSphere infrastructure, but also your Windows-based environment from a single centralized console. You can use the PowerGUI script editor to write your PowerShell scripts. You can download it from `http://software.dell.com/products/powergui-freeware/`.

PowerGUI is a friendly tool especially useful for people who don't know much about PowerShell scripting. The following screenshot shows the homepage:

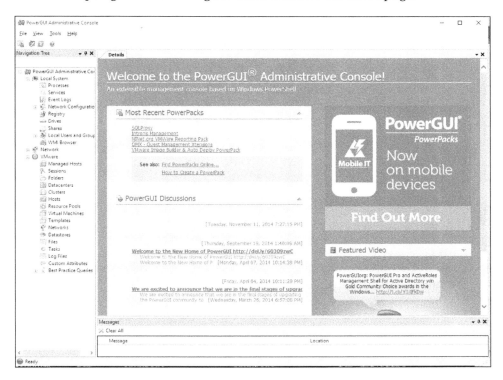

Download the PowerGUI from the previously mentioned link and double click on the downloaded setup file to start the installation wizard.

1. On the **Select Features** screen of the PowerGUI setup, everything is selected in the default installation.

2. Click on **Next** to install the PowerGUI.

3. Installation is done and it was pretty straight forward. Now, it's time to load PowerPacks to extend the PowerGUI functionality. Use the URL that follows to download the **VMware Community PowerPack**. You can find more PowerPacks by searching in the search box as well: http://en.community. dell.com/techcenter/powergui/m/powerpacks/20438900.

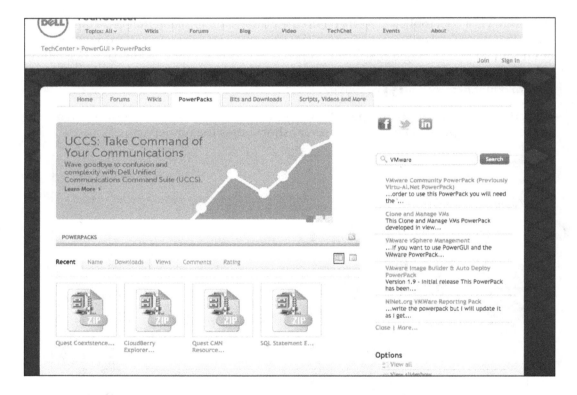

4. It will download a .zip file that contains a file with a PowerPack extension. Extract the file in the directory that you want to.

5. Click on the PowerPack Manager icon (take a look at the following screenshot):

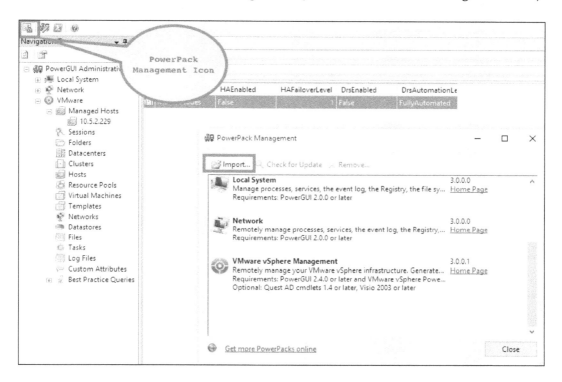

6. Click on **Import** to browse the recently downloaded PowerPack. Then, click on **Close**. The newly imported PowerPack will be automatically shown in the left pane. From there, you can browse and perform the management tasks.

Using the VMware Community PowerPack

Let's have a quick overview of our recently added VMware Community PowerPack. Perform the following steps:

1. Expand the VMware icon on the left pane.

2. Click on **Managed Hosts** and then click on **Add managed host...** on the **Actions** pane.

3. The **Add managed host... Paramenters** window will open, as shown in the following figure. Enter your vCenter Server host name or IP address.

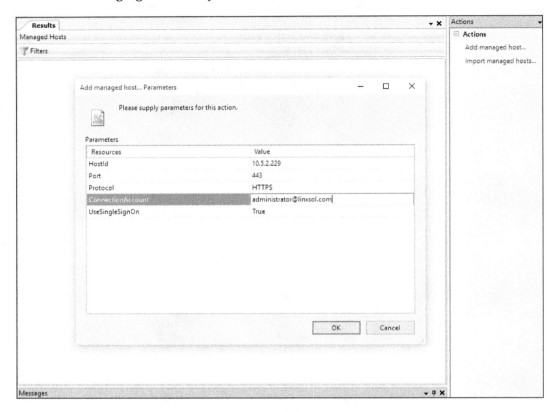

4. Enter the user name that you use to log in to your vCenter Server in **ConnectionAccount** and click on **OK**.

5. The host will be added to **Managed Hosts**. You can right click on it or you can choose **Connect...** from the **Action** pane to connect it:

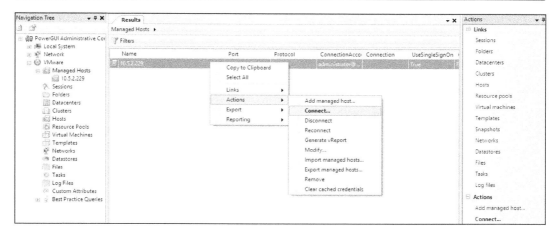

6. Once prompted, enter the details in the **Password** field for your account, as shown in the figure that follows:

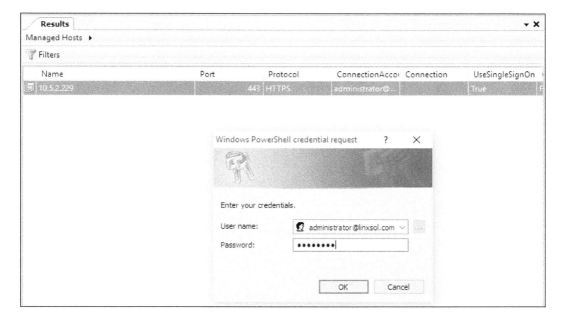

7. Click on **Session** on the left pane to see the current sessions in the vCenter Server:

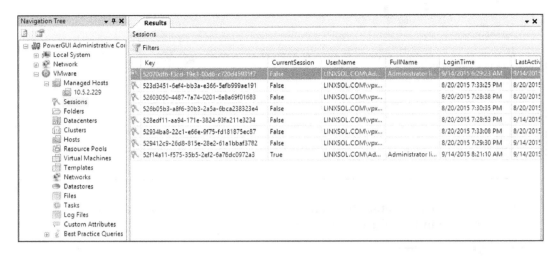

8. Click on **Datacenters** to see the available datacenters in your vCenter Server. In the same way, you can perform different actions on the object shown in the screenshot that follows, in the connected vSphere infrastructure:

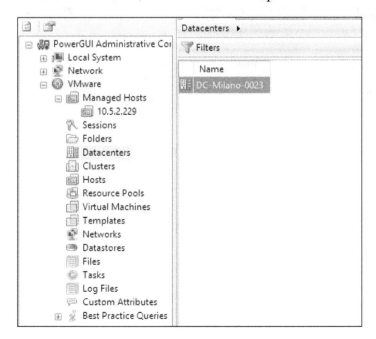

Summary

You can use PowerGUI to perform your management tasks from a single console and not only that you can also run different ready to use queries for finding different information about your vSphere infrastructure.

B
Installing VMware vRealize Operations Manager

The VMware vRealize Operations Manager helps you ensure the availability and management of your infrastructure and applications across Amazon, vSphere, physical hardware, and Hyper-V. You can monitor your applications, network devices, and storage from a single service console and apply different kinds of guided policies to control and optimize the performance of your infrastructure.

Deploying the VMware vRealize Operations Manager is an easy and simple task. You can download it from `http://myvmware.com`.

1. Right click on your vCenter Server from the vSphere web client and select **Deploy OVF Template...**, as shown in the following screenshot:

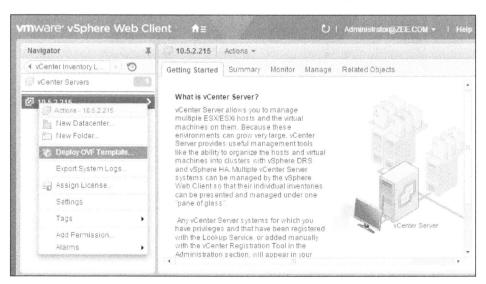

2. In **Select source**, click on **Local file**, and then, click on the **Browse** button to browse the vRealize Operations Manager Appliance file, and once done, click on **Next**:

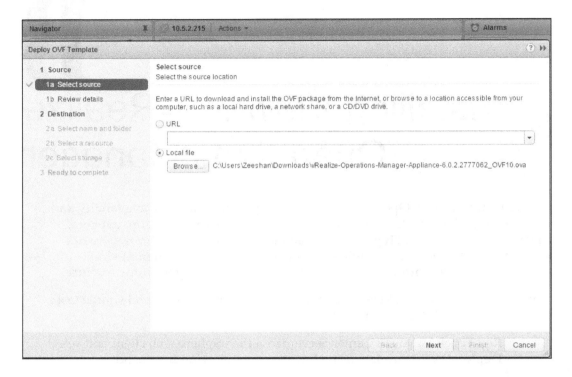

3. In the next window, you can review the details, the vRealize Operations Manager Appliance version number, its size, and its size on the disk. Review this information and click on **Next**:

4. Accept **License Agreement**, as shown in the following screenshot, and click on **Next**:

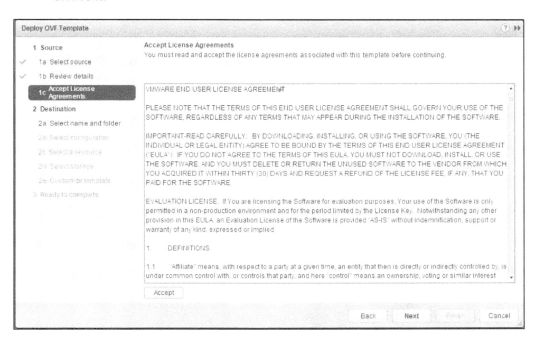

5. In the next wizard window, in **Select name and folder**, choose the Data Center or a folder that you want to deploy vRealize Operations Manager Appliance in, as shown next:

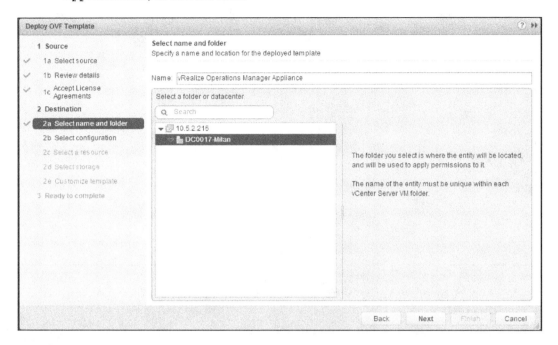

6. Depending on your infrastructure needs, you can choose to deploy a different configuration from **Small**, **Medium**, **Large**, **Remote Collector (Standard)**, **Remote Collector (Large)**, and **Extra Small**. We will choose **Small** here, and then click on **Next**:

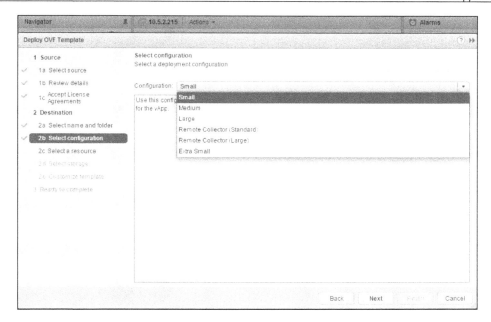

7. Choose a cluster or vSphere host, in which you want to host your vRealize Operations Manager Appliance, and from the **Select a resource** wizard window, and click on **Next**:

8. From the **Select storage** wizard window, you can select the type of storage you want. Here, we have chosen **Thin Provision**; you can leave the default **VM Storage Policy** field as is and choose the datastore that you want to store the appliance in:

9. In the next window, choose the network you would like to connect to and the IP allocation type, in my case it is static, and then click on **Next**:

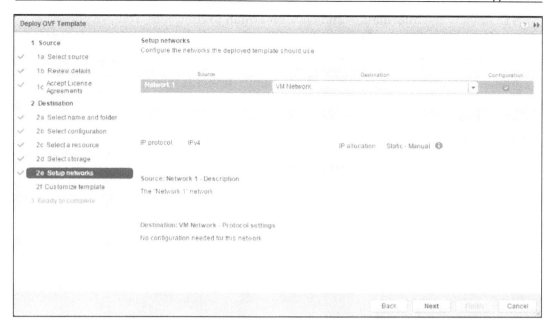

10. Add the time zone, IP address/subnet information, and DNS address and click on **Next**:

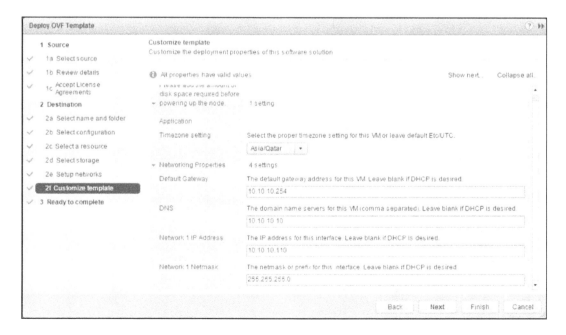

11. Review the information and click on **Finish** to complete. You can choose to **Power on after deployment** by ticking the check box, or you can manually start the appliance later on:

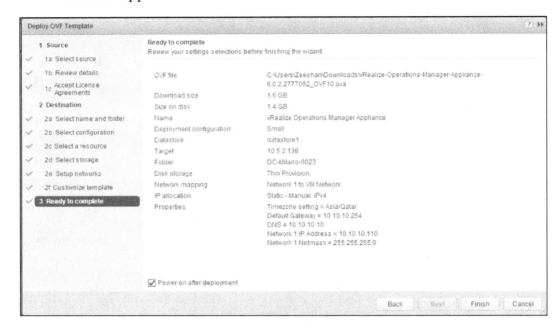

12. Browse `https://IP-Address/vcops-web-ent/login.action` to log in to vRealize Operations Manager:

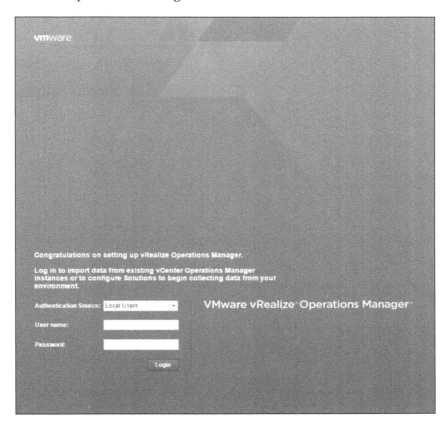

13. When you log in for first time, vRealize Operations Manager asks if you want to configure a **New Environment**, or you want to import an existing environment by selecting **Import Environment**.

14. Choose **New Cluster** and click on **Next**:

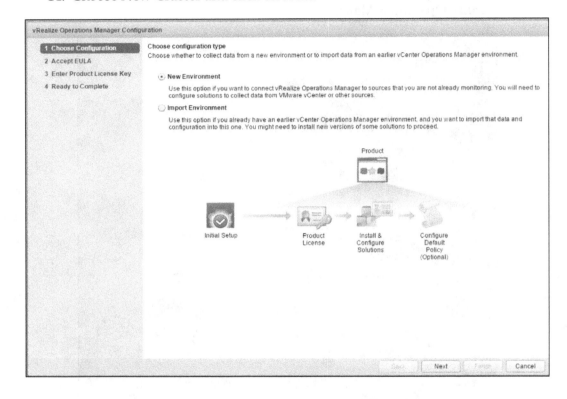

15. Click on accept for **Accept the Agreement**:

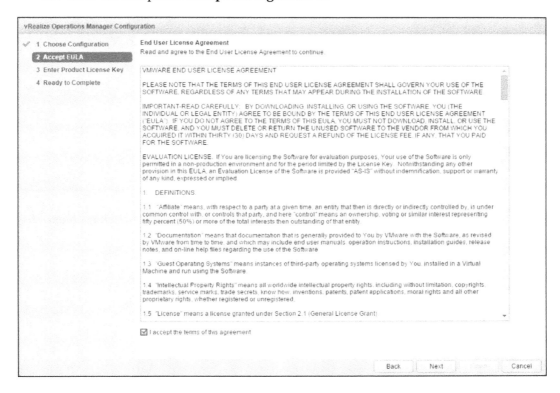

16. Enter the **Product Key** if you have purchased it, or you can try it as an evaluation and click on **Next**:

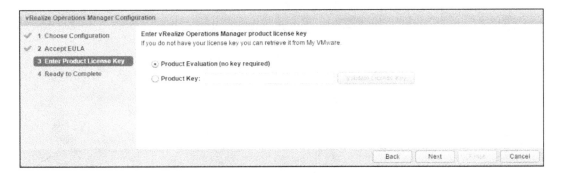

17. Set up the **Administrator** user by choosing a password and click on **Next**.

18. Click on **Finish** to complete the wizard:

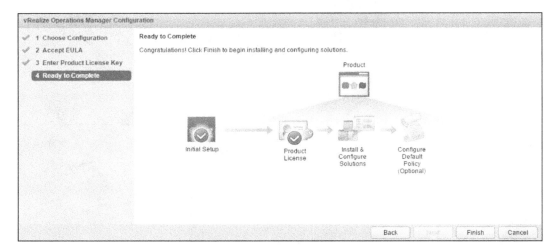

Summary

This concludes the installation of VMware vRealize Operations Manager. Next you can start using it to automate IT operations management for your vSphere infrastructure.

C
Power CLI - A Basic Reference

Log in to `https://my.vmware.com/web/vmware/login` and download the VMware vSphere PowerCLI 6.0 release 1 or release 2. We have used the PowerCLI 6.0 R 1 in this appendix, but R 2 is publically available to download:

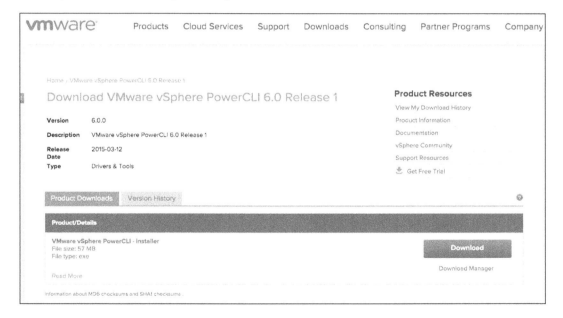

Double click on the downloaded file to start the installation wizard, as shown in the following screenshot:

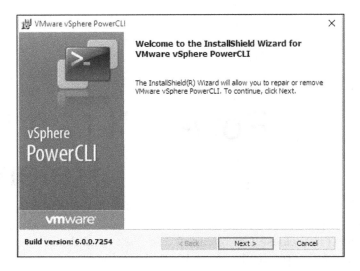

Click on **Next** and accept the following agreement:

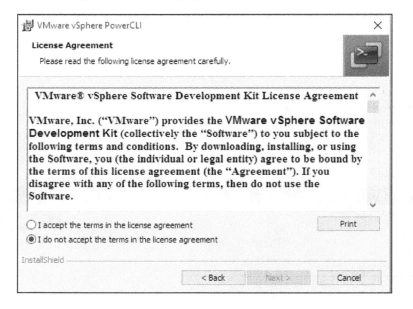

In the next window, you can choose the features that you would like to install. In previous versions of PowerCLI, vCloud or vCD PowerCLI, these features are not installed by default. In PowerCLI 6.0, vCloud Air/vCD PowerCLI is already enabled by default. We will install vCD PowerCLI as we have a vCloud Director installed. You can choose to disable it according to your environment. Click on **Next**:

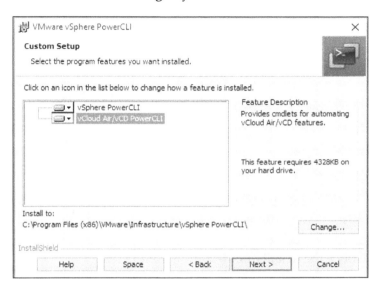

And then, click on **Install**:

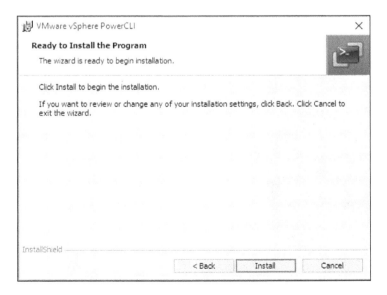

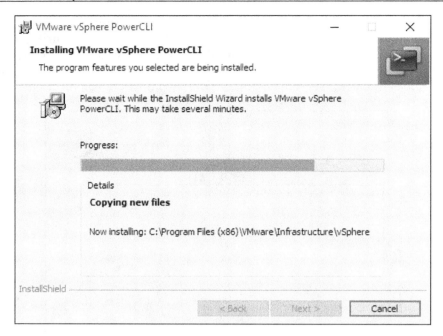

Click on **Finish** once the installation wizard is completed:

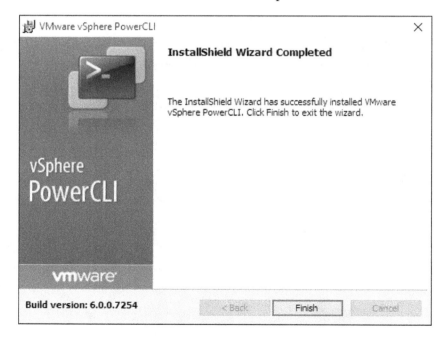

Open the installed vSphere PowerCLI via the shortcut on your desktop. You will be presented with a welcome message and some basic commands as a reference to start with, as shown in the following screenshot:

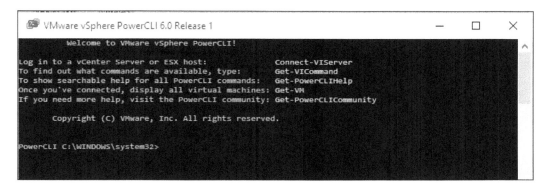

Before we start executing scripts or running commands, we need to check the execution policy. To check that, we can type the following command in our PowerCLI of vSphere or Windows PowerShell:

`Get-ExecutionPolicy`

If it is set to restricted, which is the default policy, you will not need to execute scripts. To enable it, type the following, as shown in the next screenshot, and type Y to accept it:

`Set-ExecutionPolicy -ExecutionPolicy RemoteSigned`

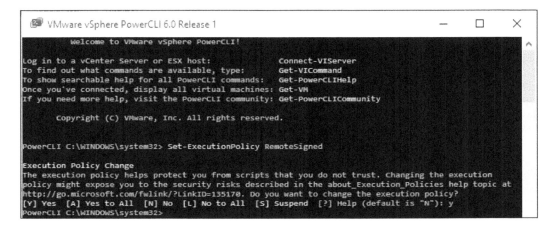

To connect to a vCenter Server, type the following:

```
Connect-VIServer 10.5.2.229
```

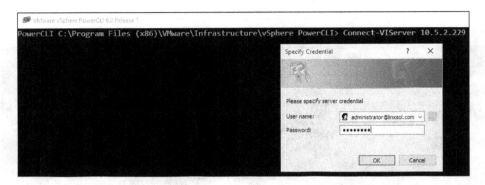

Once prompted, enter your username and password, and click on **OK**. You will see the output in the PowerCLI of the vCenter Server Name or IP address, the port it is connected to, and the user name that is being used for the connection:

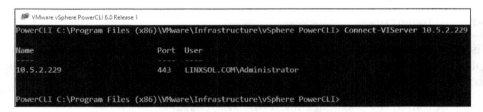

You can see the list of recently connected vCenter Servers or vSphere hosts by typing the following command:

```
Connect-VIServer - Menu
```

Now the vCenter Server is connected to retrieve a list of virtual machines currently hosted. To do this, you can type the following:

```
Get-VM
```

You can see the list of virtual machines in the following screenshot:

To get more information about the hard disk of the vCenter005 virtual machine, type the following:

```
Get-VM -Name vCenter005 | Get-HardDisk
```

To list modules, type the following:

```
Get-Module -ListAvailable VMware*
```

The Get-Module command will list all the available modules to be imported in PowerCLI.

Summary

This concludes our last appendix. Power CLI is a very useful tool for system engineers who like to automate their daily tasks of vSphere infrastructure. For digging more deeper into PowerCLI you can follow the documentation.

Index

PowerGUI
  about 209
  installation wizard, starting 210, 211
  URL, for downloading 209
PowerPacks
  URL 210
power tools
  troubleshooting with 5
precise communication 3
PSA troubleshooting 144, 145
PVLANs
  verifying 120

R

resignaturing 180, 181
resxtop
  using 36-38, 61
Return on Investment (ROI) 4
Root Cause Analysis (RCA) 4
route
  deleting 135
Runtime Name 157

S

SAN display problems 181
SAN performance
  troubleshooting 182
secondary PVLANs
  verifying 120
Secure Shell Session (SSH) 29
Security Assertion Markup Language
      (SAML) 189
SIOC logging
  about 90
  enabling 90, 91
SNMP agents
  configuring, from PowerCLI 97, 98
  tuning 96
SNMP traps
  configuring, for continuous monitoring 94
  configuring, with vMA 95
SSL certificates
  implementing, for ESXi 194
stdout
  logs, generating on 30

storage adapters 142
Storage Array Type Plugin (SATP) 146
storage devices
  identifying 155-158
  listing, from vMA 159-161
Storage DRS
  common errors 83
Storage I/O Control (SIOC)
  about 88, 143
  enabling 89
storage log files
  about 143
  DRMDump 144
  hostd.log file 143
  storageRM.log file 143, 144
  vmkernel.log file 144
storage metrics
  about 58
  ABRTS/s 60
  CMDS/s 59
  CONS/s 60
  DAVG/cmd 59
  GAVG/cmd 60
  KAVG/cmd 59
  MBREAD/s 60
  MBWRTN/s 60
  QAVG/cmd 60
  QUED 60
  READS/s 60
  RESETS/s 60
  WRITES/s 60
storage module troubleshooting 172, 173
storage path masking 152
storageRM.log file 143, 144
SUSE Linux Enterprise Server 11 SP1
      64-bit 9
Symantec Dynamic Multi-Pathing
  URL 145
syslog server
  setting up, manually 21
  setting up, PowerCLI used 20
  vMA, configuring as 14-16
systematic flowchart, for storage
      troubleshooting
  reference link 158
systems
  accessing, from vMA 18, 19

Thank you for buying
VMware vSphere Troubleshooting

About Packt Publishing

Packt, pronounced 'packed', published its first book, *Mastering phpMyAdmin for Effective MySQL Management*, in April 2004, and subsequently continued to specialize in publishing highly focused books on specific technologies and solutions.

Our books and publications share the experiences of your fellow IT professionals in adapting and customizing today's systems, applications, and frameworks. Our solution-based books give you the knowledge and power to customize the software and technologies you're using to get the job done. Packt books are more specific and less general than the IT books you have seen in the past. Our unique business model allows us to bring you more focused information, giving you more of what you need to know, and less of what you don't.

Packt is a modern yet unique publishing company that focuses on producing quality, cutting-edge books for communities of developers, administrators, and newbies alike. For more information, please visit our website at www.packtpub.com.

About Packt Enterprise

In 2010, Packt launched two new brands, Packt Enterprise and Packt Open Source, in order to continue its focus on specialization. This book is part of the Packt Enterprise brand, home to books published on enterprise software – software created by major vendors, including (but not limited to) IBM, Microsoft, and Oracle, often for use in other corporations. Its titles will offer information relevant to a range of users of this software, including administrators, developers, architects, and end users.

Writing for Packt

We welcome all inquiries from people who are interested in authoring. Book proposals should be sent to author@packtpub.com. If your book idea is still at an early stage and you would like to discuss it first before writing a formal book proposal, then please contact us; one of our commissioning editors will get in touch with you.

We're not just looking for published authors; if you have strong technical skills but no writing experience, our experienced editors can help you develop a writing career, or simply get some additional reward for your expertise.

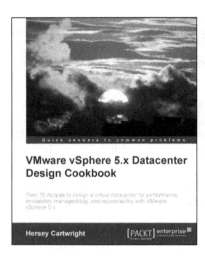

VMware vSphere 5.x Datacenter Design Cookbook

Over 70 recipes to design a virtual datacenter for performance, availability, manageability, and recoverability with VMware vSphere 5.x

Hersey Cartwright

VMware vSphere 5.x Datacenter Design Cookbook

ISBN: 978-1-78217-700-5   Paperback: 260 pages

Over 70 recipes to design a virtual datacenter for performance, availability, manageability, and recoverability with VMware vSphere 5.x

1. Innovative recipes, offering numerous practical solutions when designing virtualized datacenters.

2. Identify the design factors — requirements, assumptions, constraints, and risks — by conducting stakeholder interviews and performing technical assessments.

3. Increase and guarantee performance, availability, and workload efficiency with practical steps and design considerations.

VMware vSphere 5.1 Cookbook

Over 130 task-oriented recipes to install, configure, and manage various vSphere 5.1 components

Abhilash GB

VMware vSphere 5.1 Cookbook

ISBN: 978-1-84968-402-6   Paperback: 466 pages

Over 130 task-oriented recipes to install, configure, and manage various vSphere 5.1 components

1. Install and configure vSphere 5.1 core components.

2. Learn important aspects of vSphere such as administration, security, and performance.

3. Configure vSphere Management Assistant(VMA) to run commands/scripts without the need to authenticate every attempt.

Please check **www.PacktPub.com** for information on our titles

Troubleshooting vSphere Storage

ISBN: 978-1-78217-206-2   Paperback: 150 pages

Become a master at troubleshooting and solving common storage issues in your vSphere environment

1. Identify key issues that affect vSphere storage visibility, performance, and capacity.

2. Comprehend the storage metrics and statistics that are collected in vSphere.

3. Get acquainted with the many vSphere features that can proactively protect your environment.

VMware vSphere Essentials

ISBN: 978-1-78439-875-0   Paperback: 228 pages

Efficiently virtualize your IT infrastructure with vSphere

1. Plan, deploy, and manage your vSphere environment for even the most complex IT infrastructures.

2. Familiarize yourself with vSphere infrastructure to become a skilled vSphere administrator.

3. Seamlessly configure and deploy vSphere with simple examples in this fast-paced guide.

Please check **www.PacktPub.com** for information on our titles